HEXANNE

THE TEENAGE EXORCIST

CREATED BY
EVERETTE HARTSOE

PHOTOS BY
MICHELE GREY HARTSOE

MODEL
ALYSSA KLIMEK

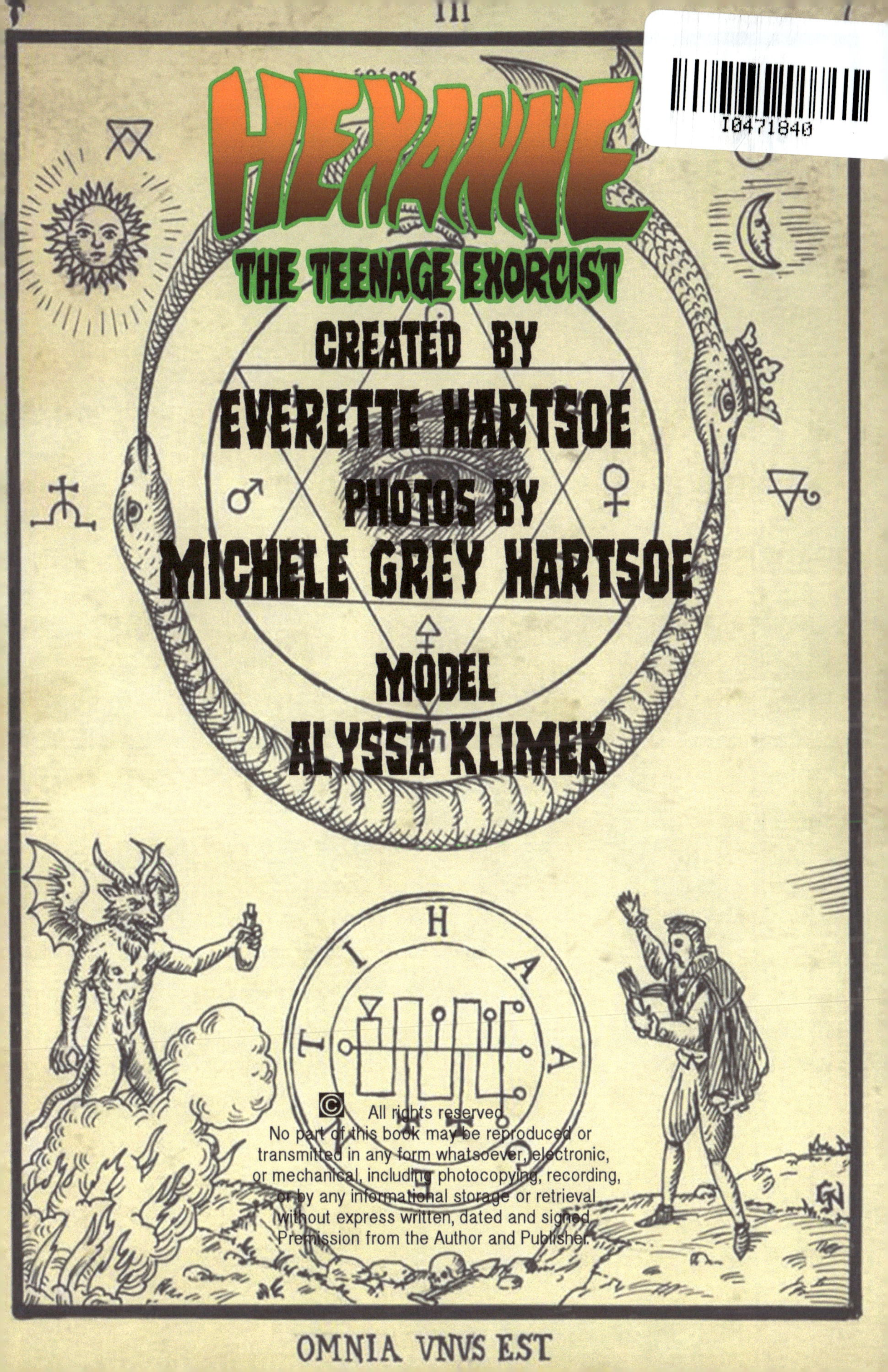

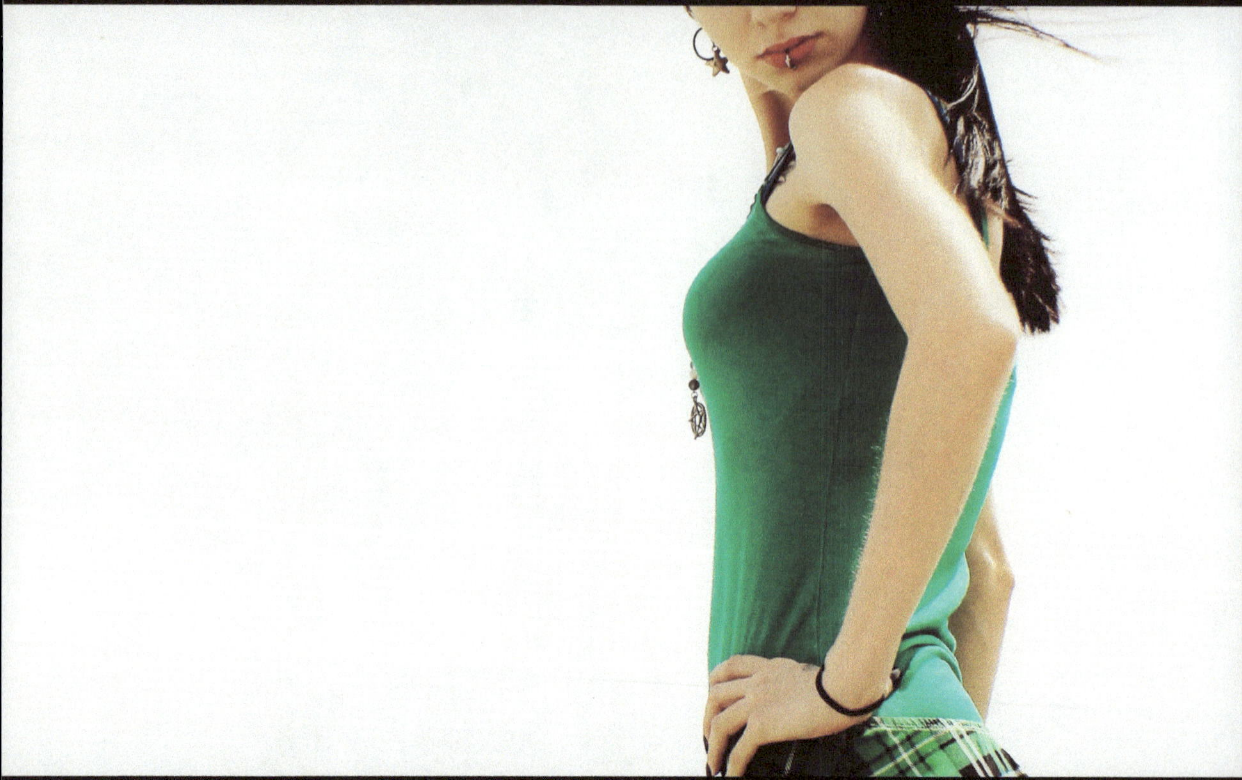

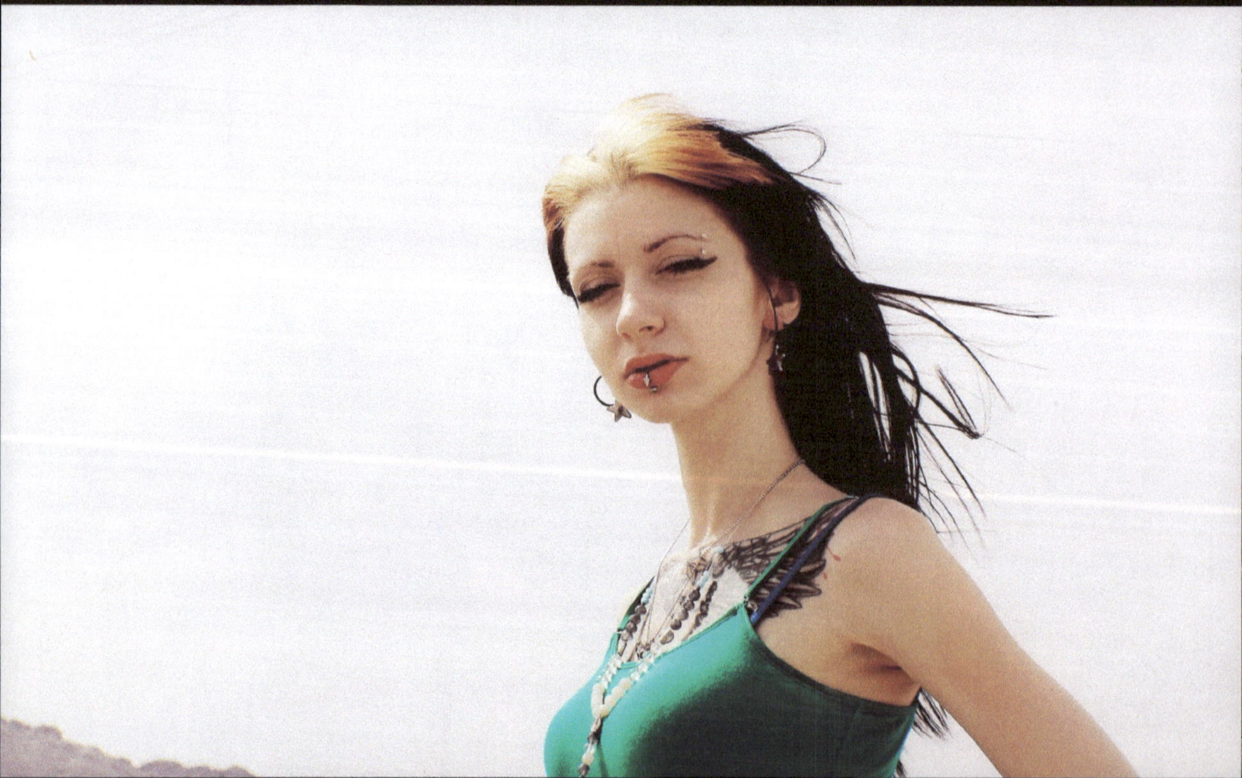

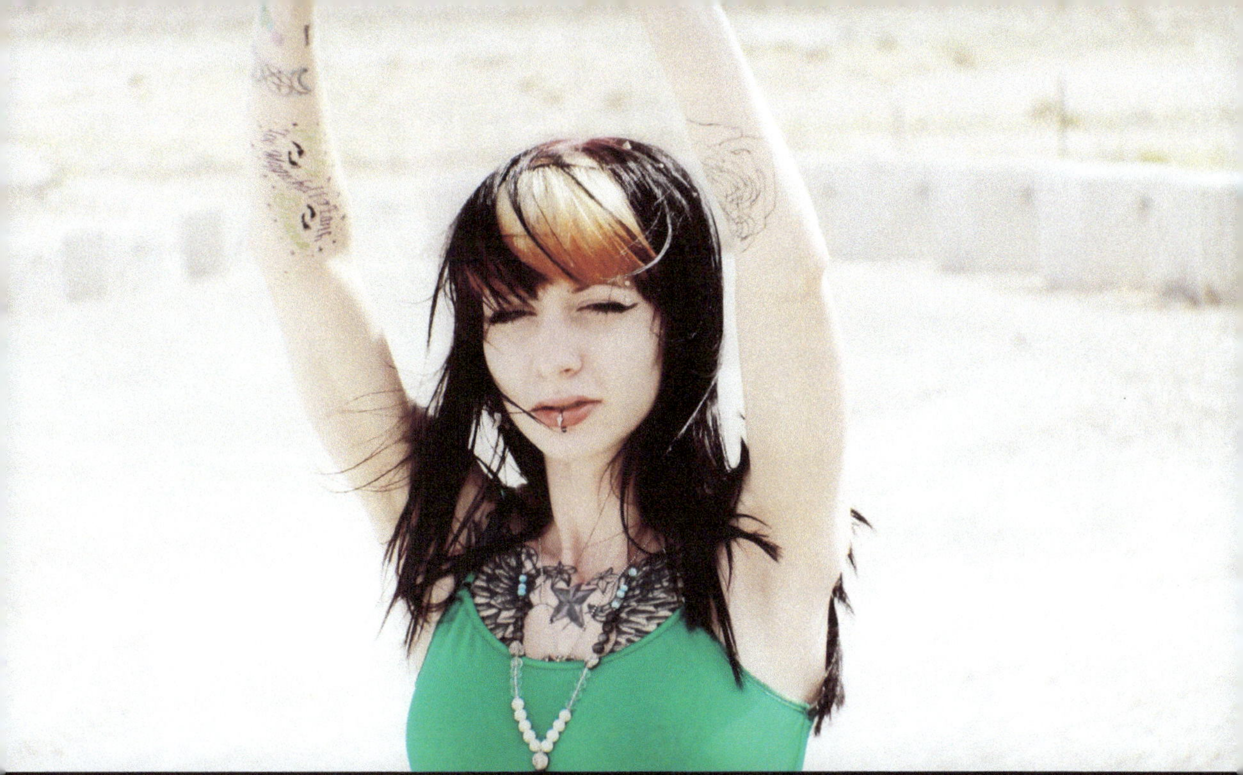

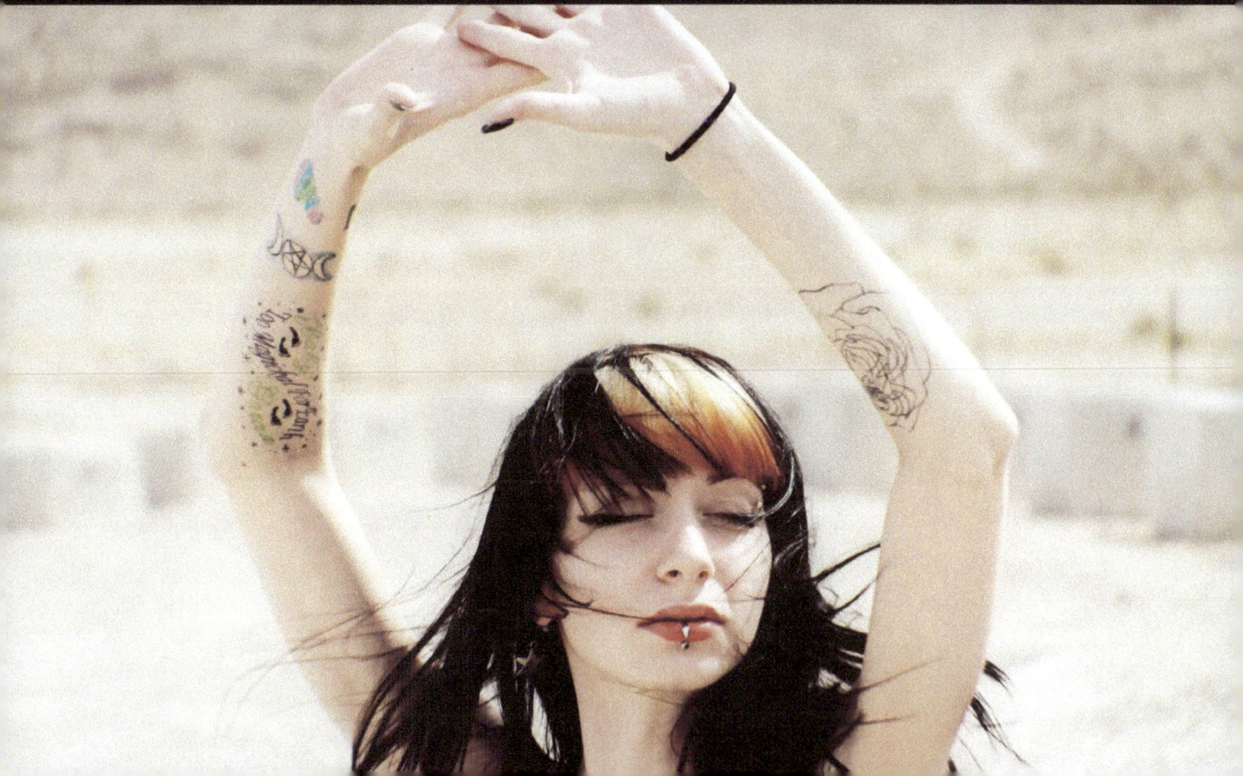

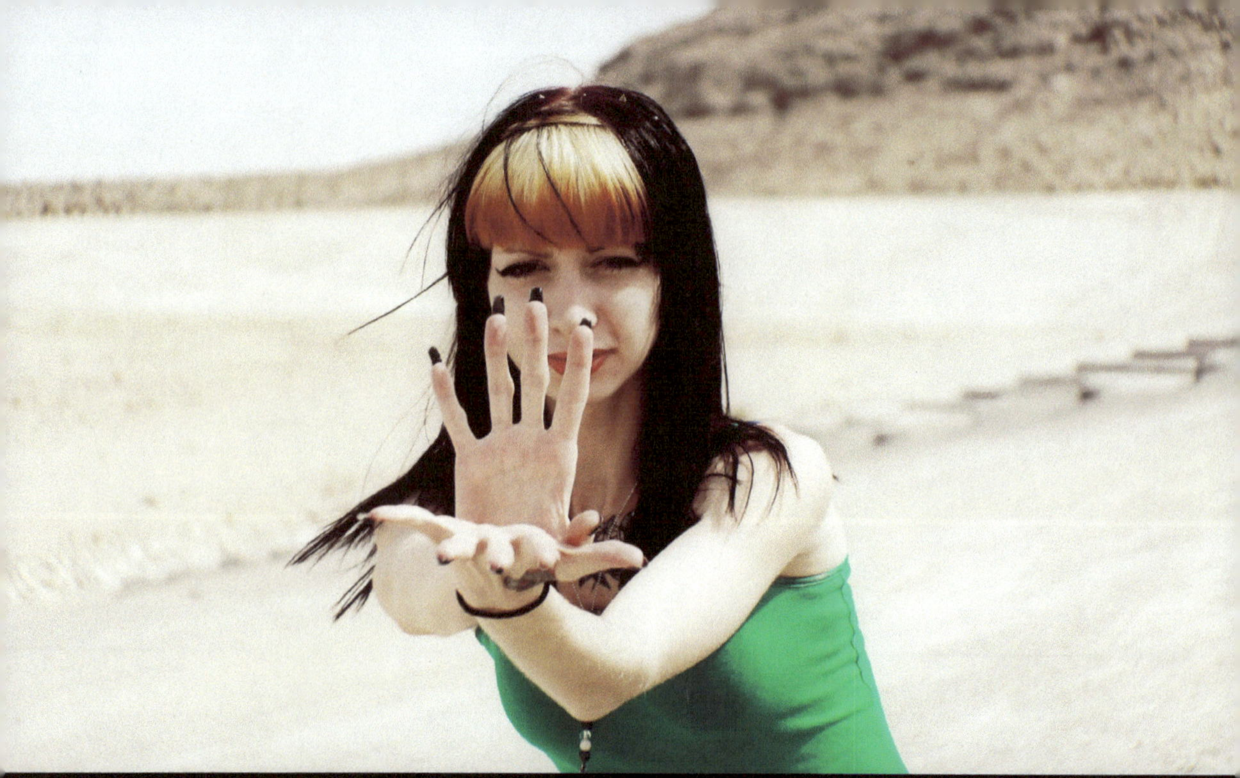

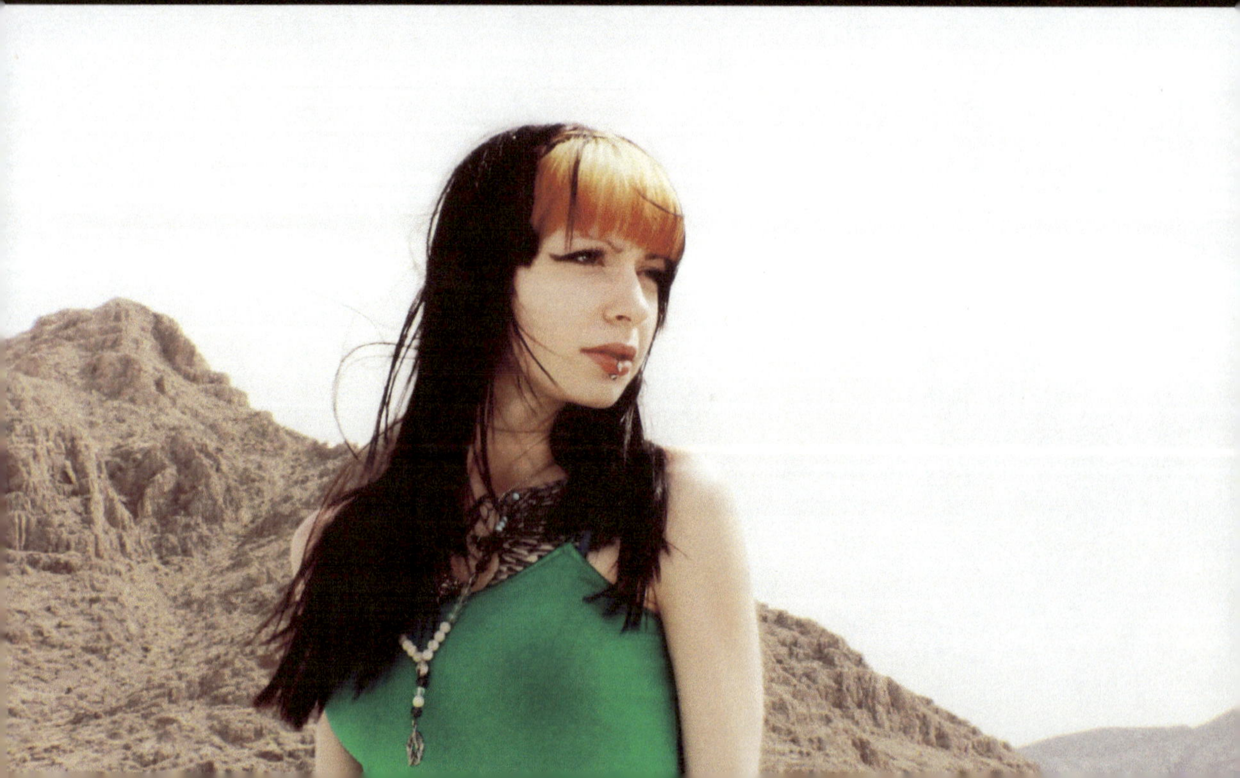

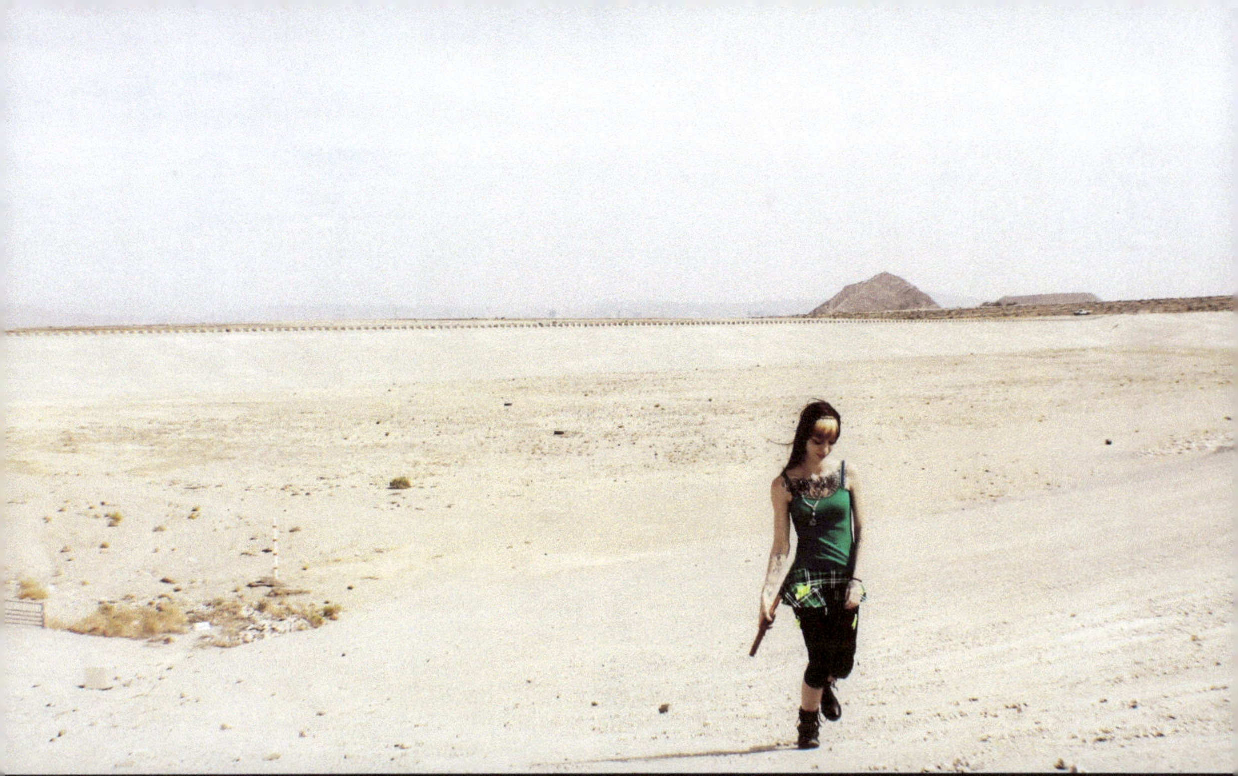

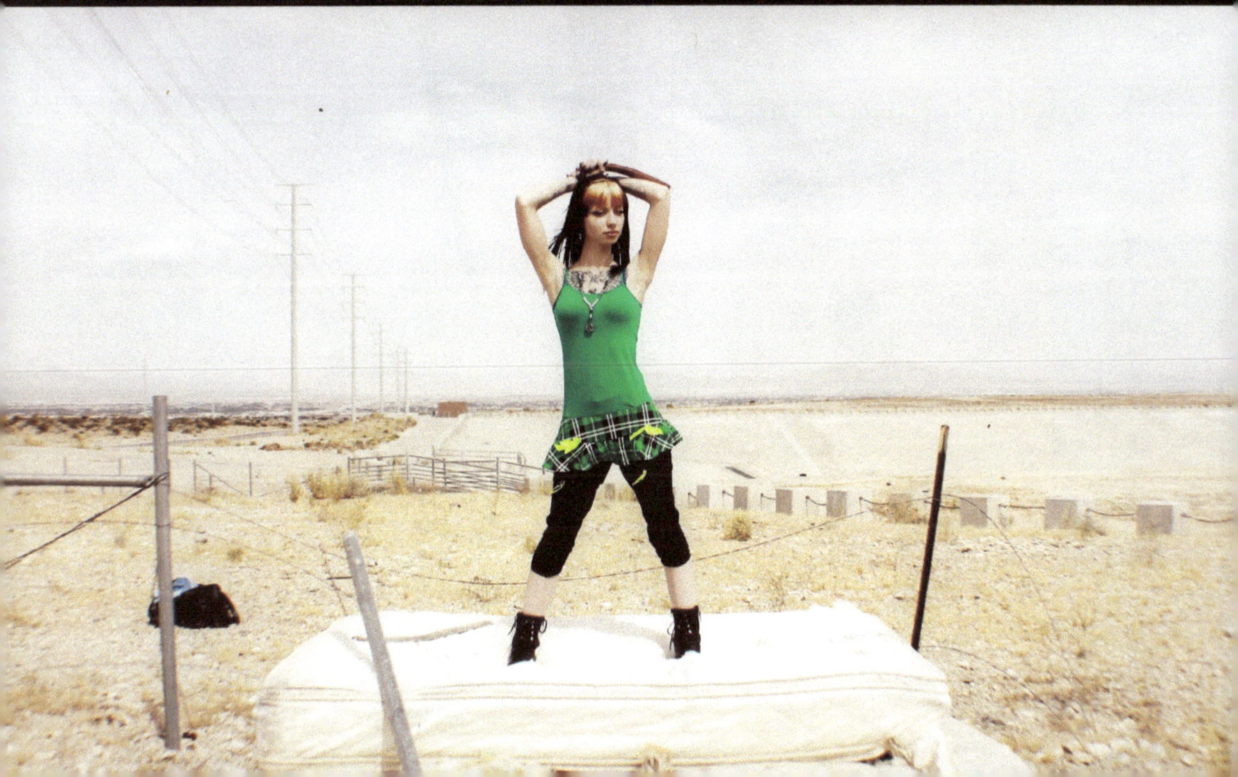

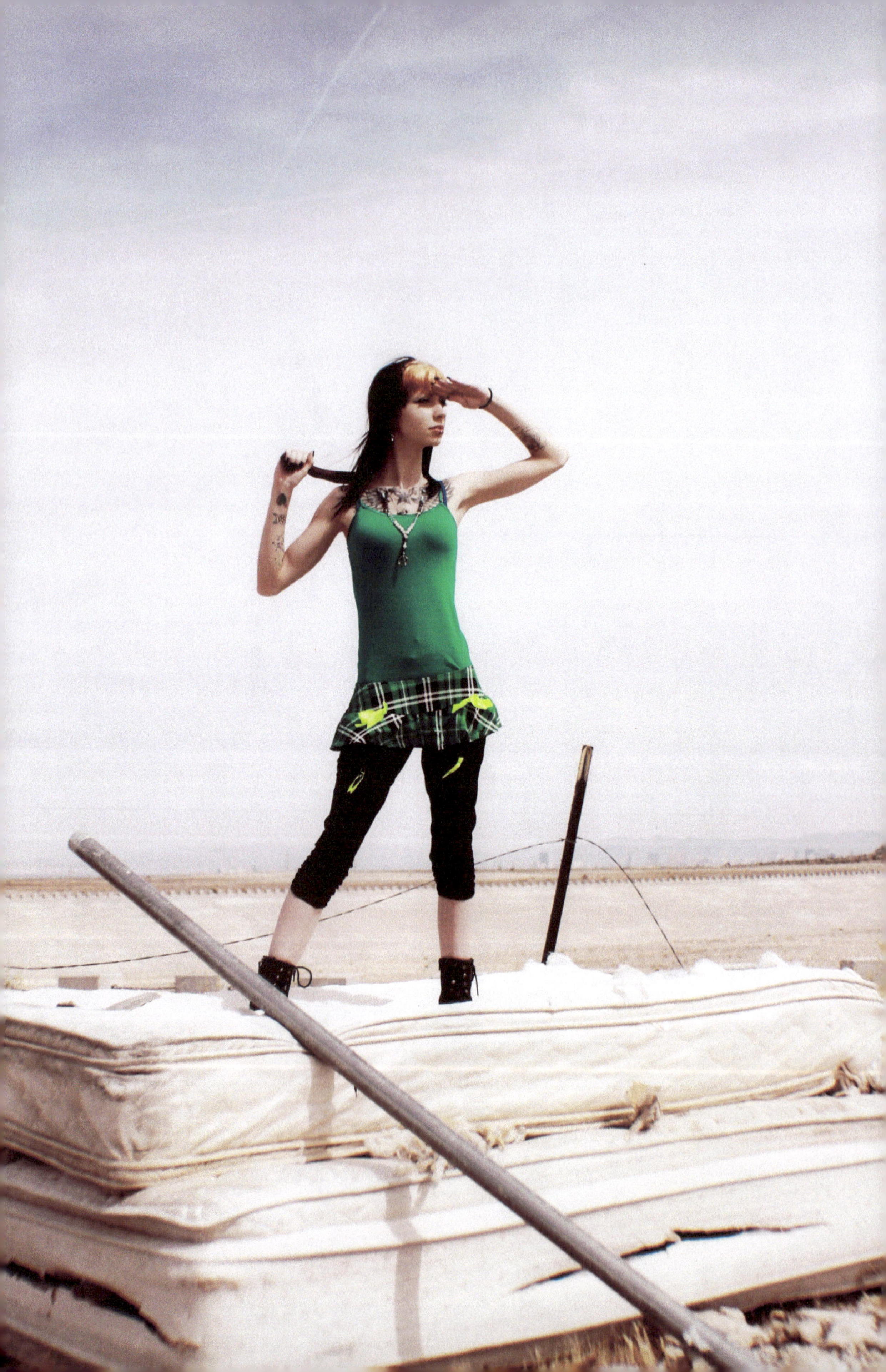

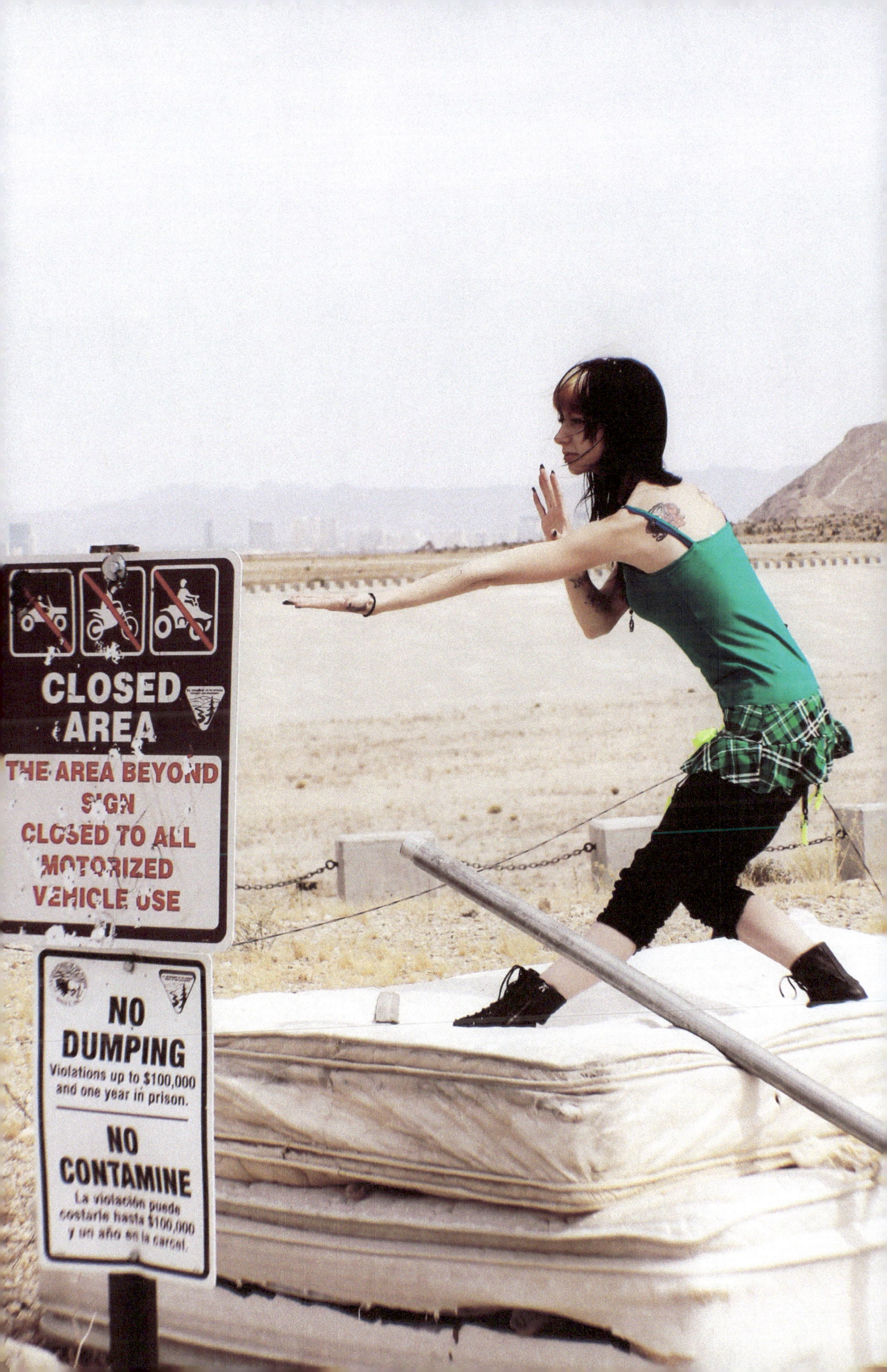
CLOSED
AREA
THE AREA BEYOND
SIGN
CLOSED TO ALL
MOTORIZED
VEHICLE USE
NO
DUMPING
Violations up to $100,000
and one year in prison.
NO
CONTAMINE
La violación puede
costarle hasta $100,000
y un año en la carcel.

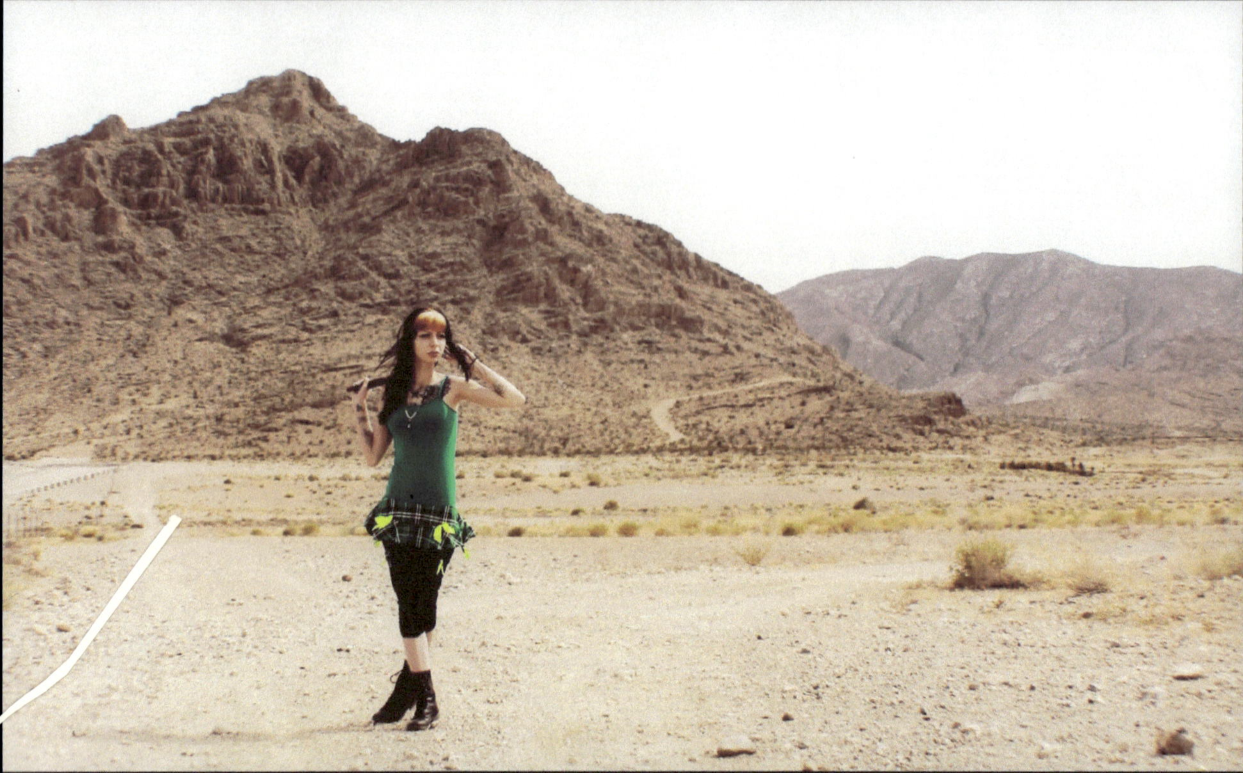

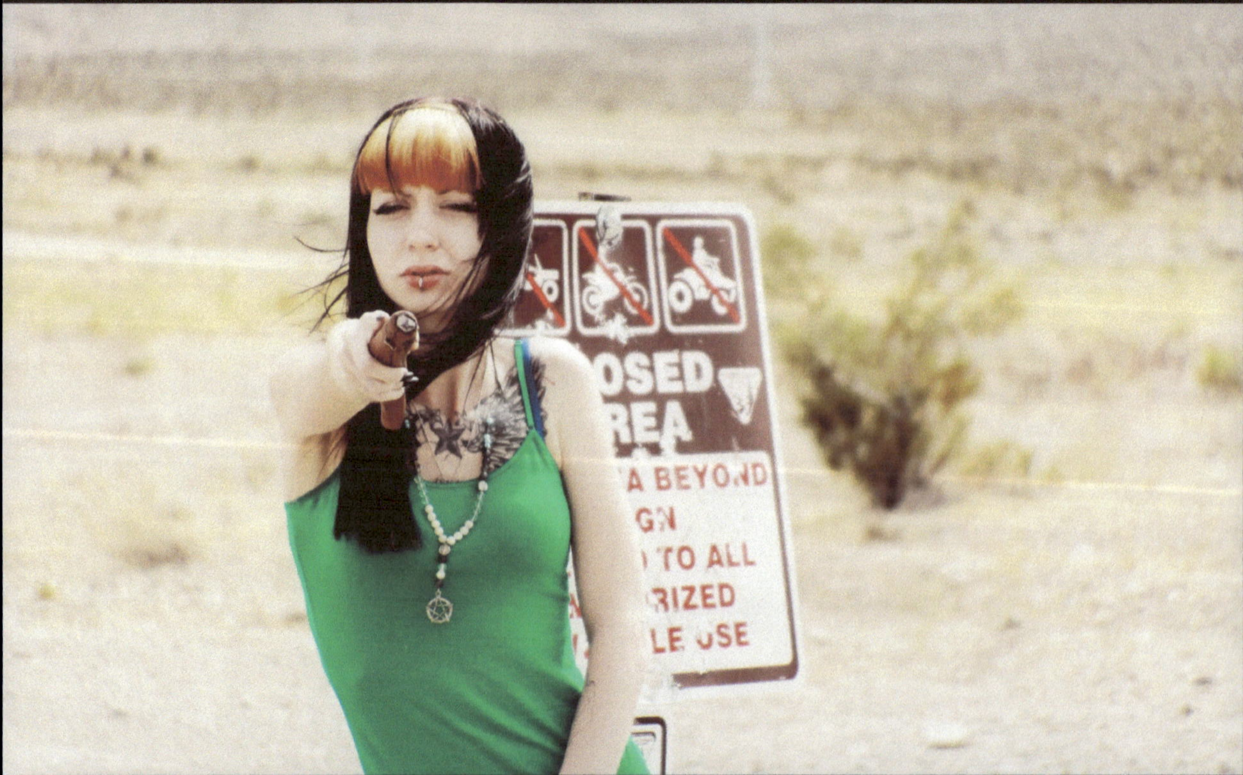
A BEYOND
TO ALL

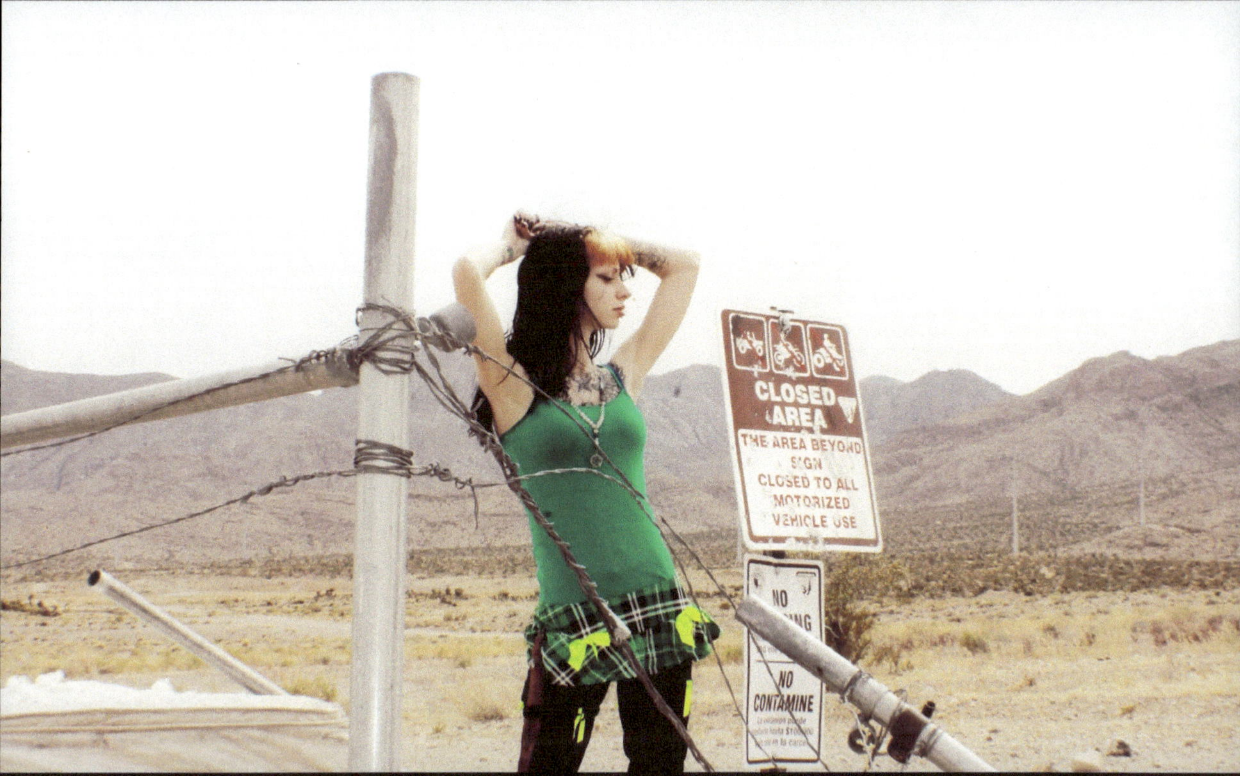
CLOSED
AREA
THE AREA BEYOND
SIGN
CLOSED TO ALL
MOTORIZED
VEHICLE USE
NO
CONTAMINE

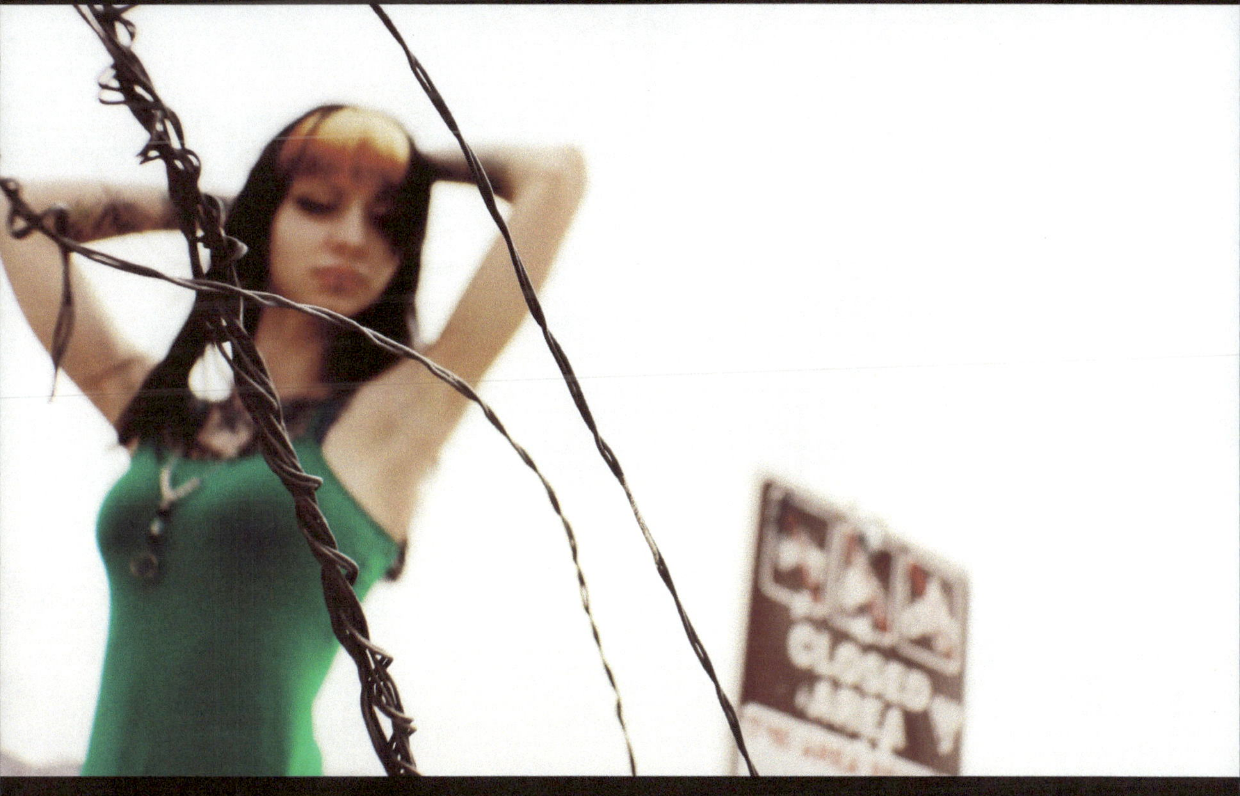

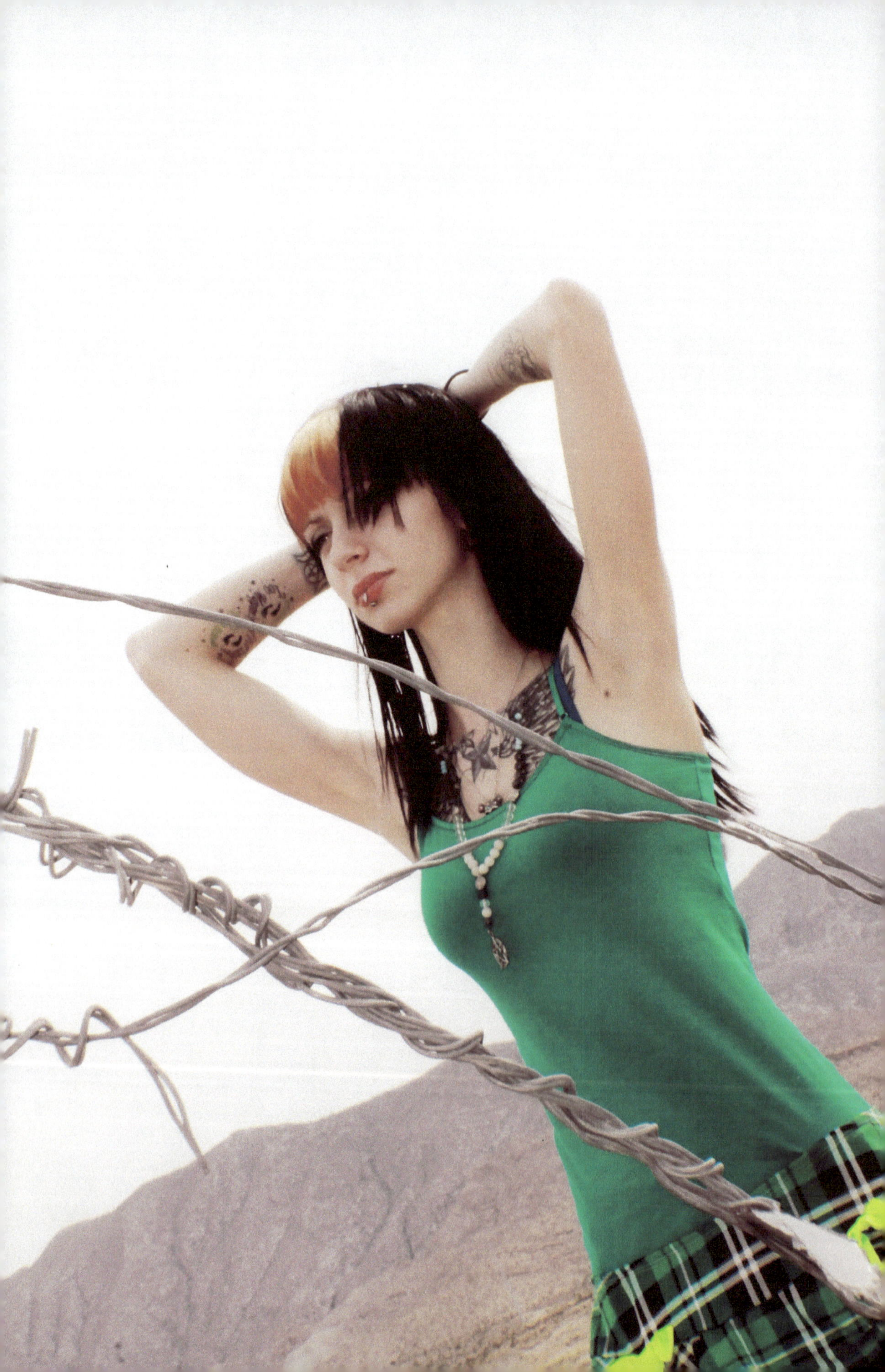

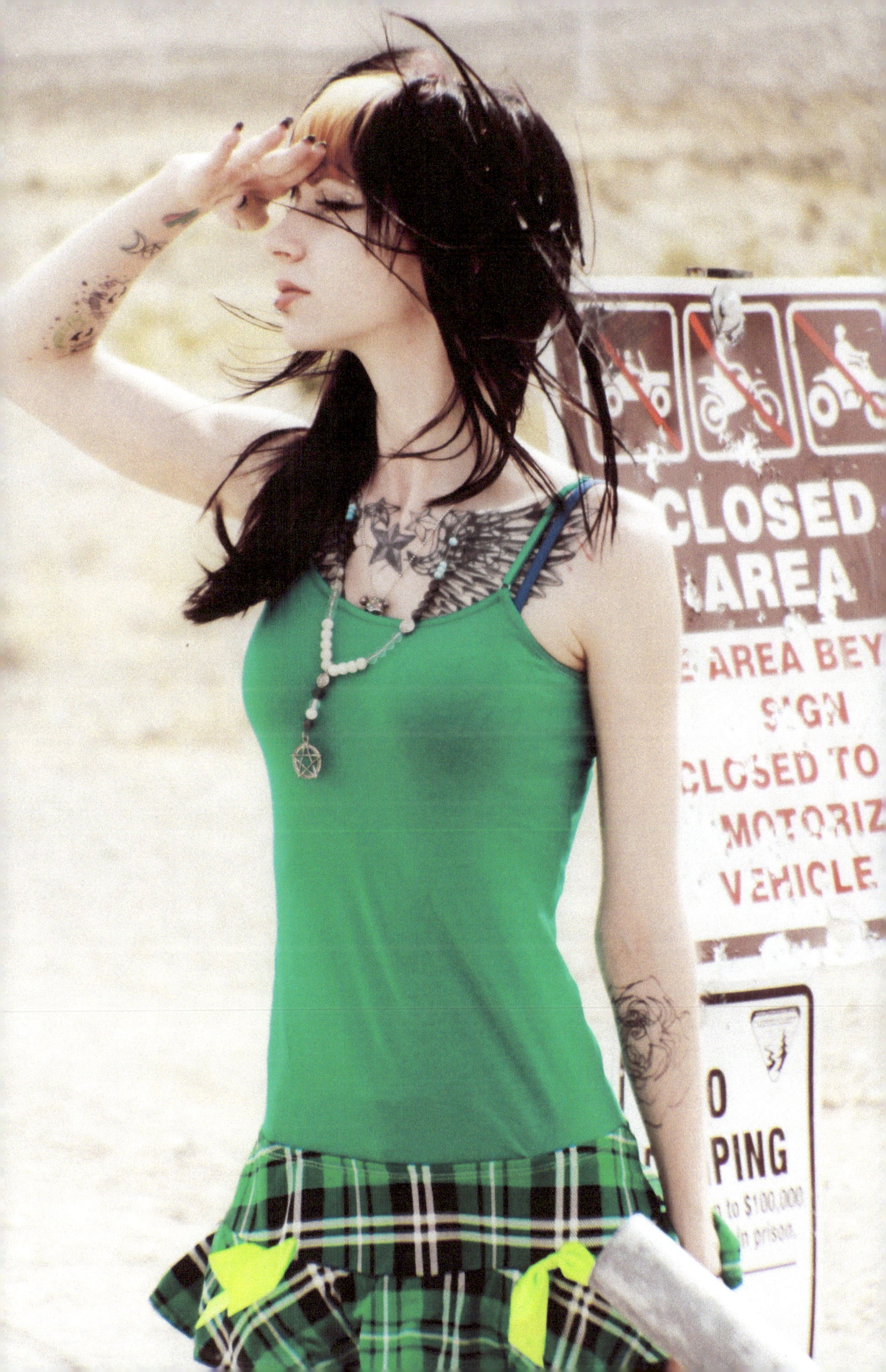
CLOSED
AREA
AREA BEY
SIGN
CLOSED TO
MOTORIZ
VEHICLE
PING
to $100,000
prison.

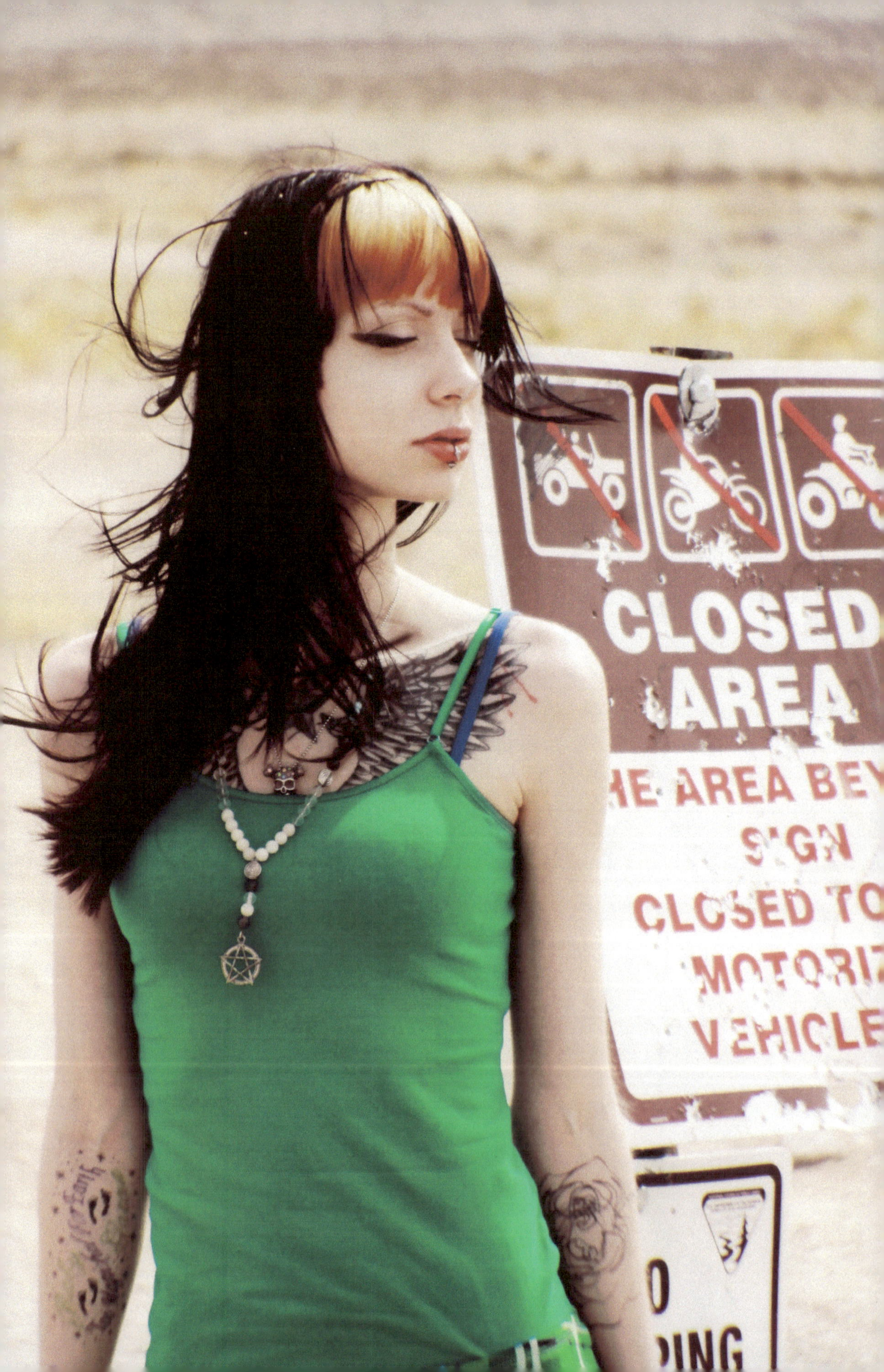

CLOSED
AREA
HE AREA BEY
SIGN
CLOSED TO
MOTORIZ
VEHICLE
PING

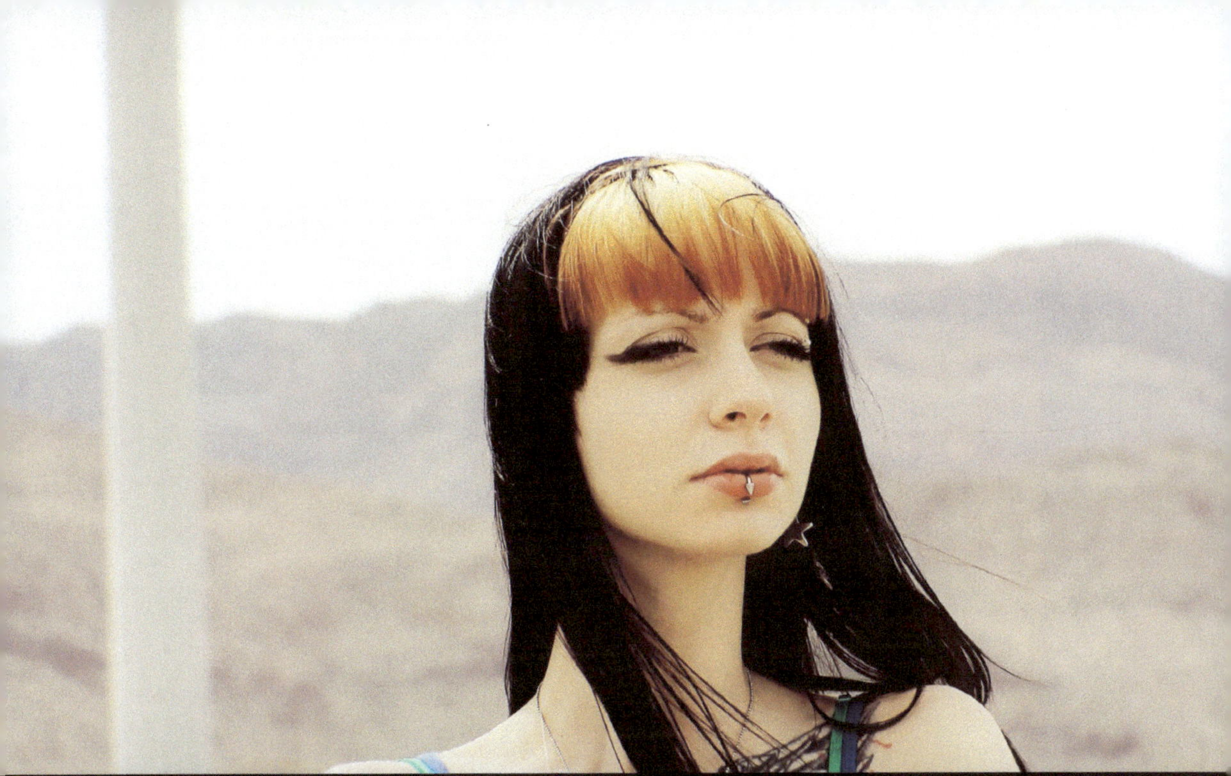

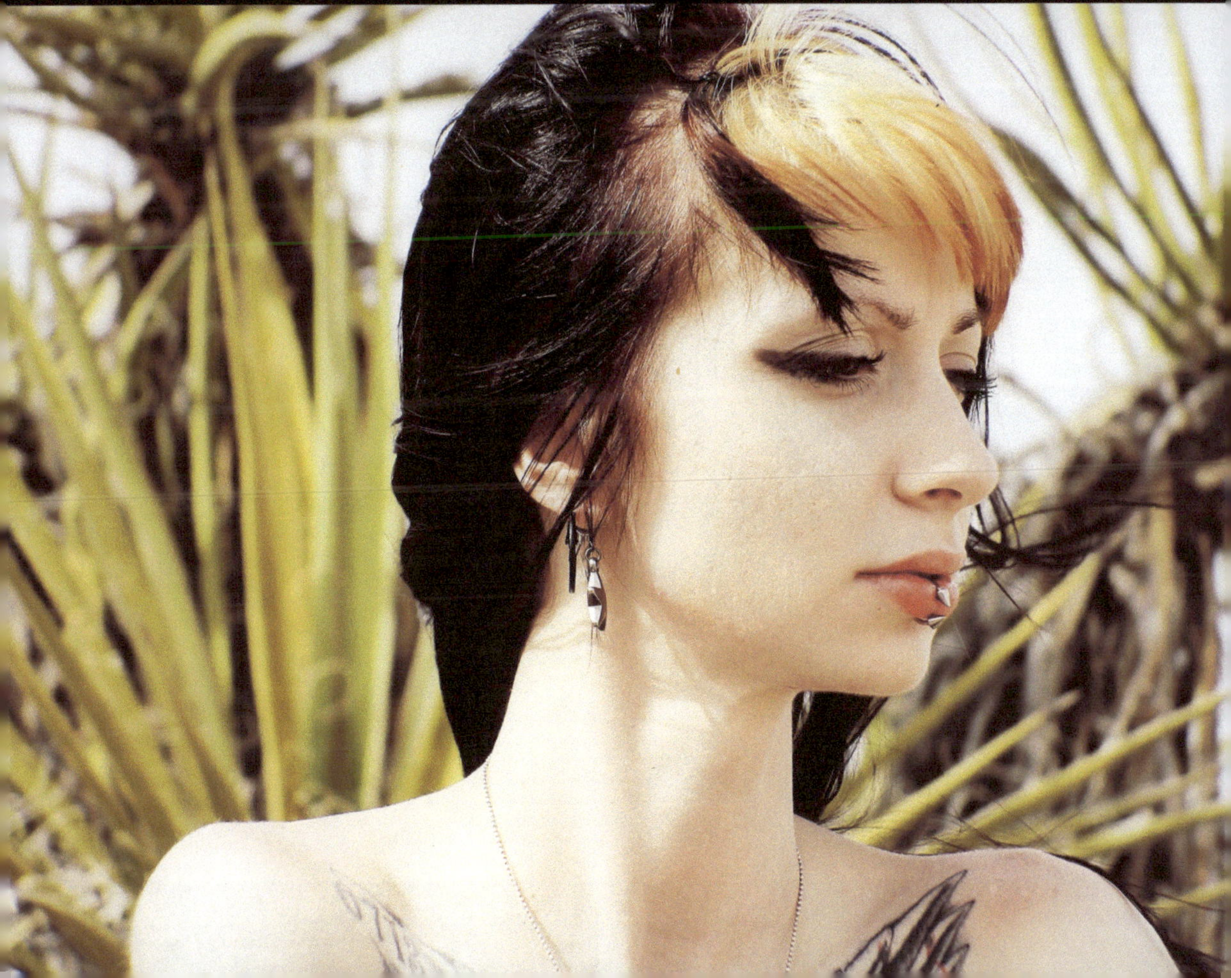

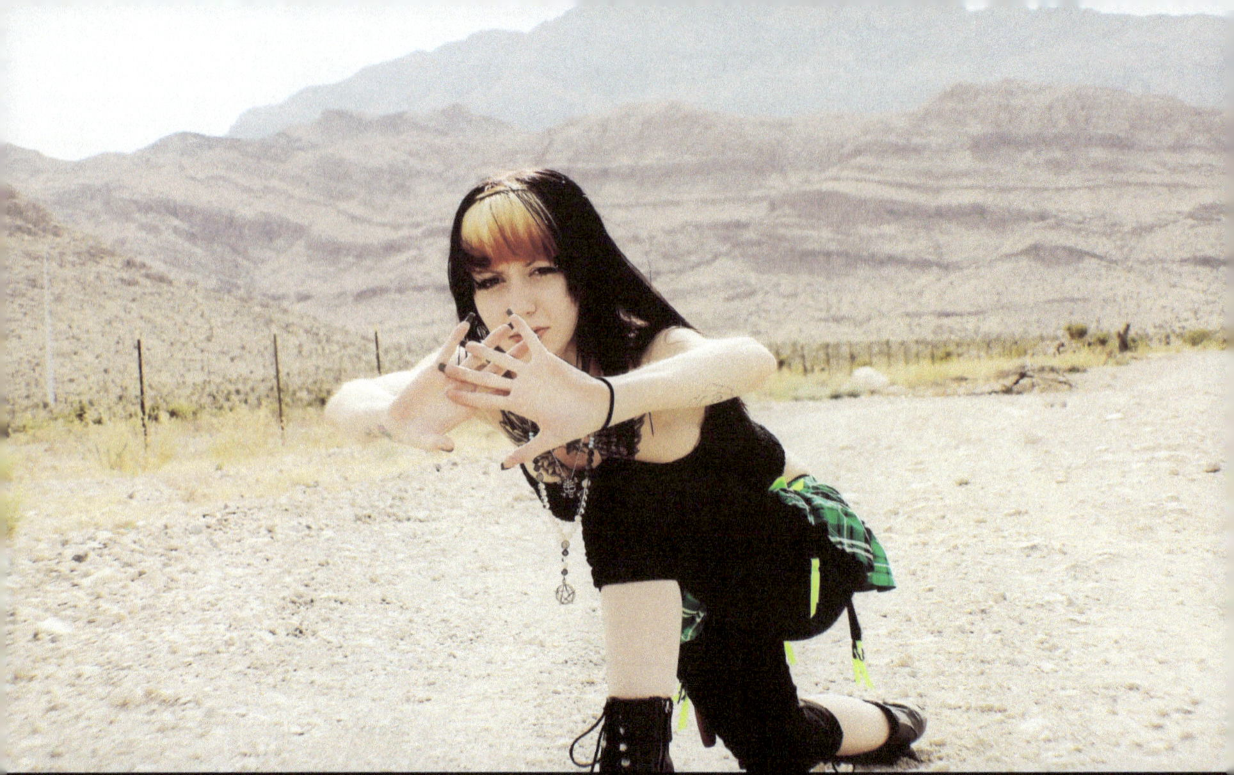

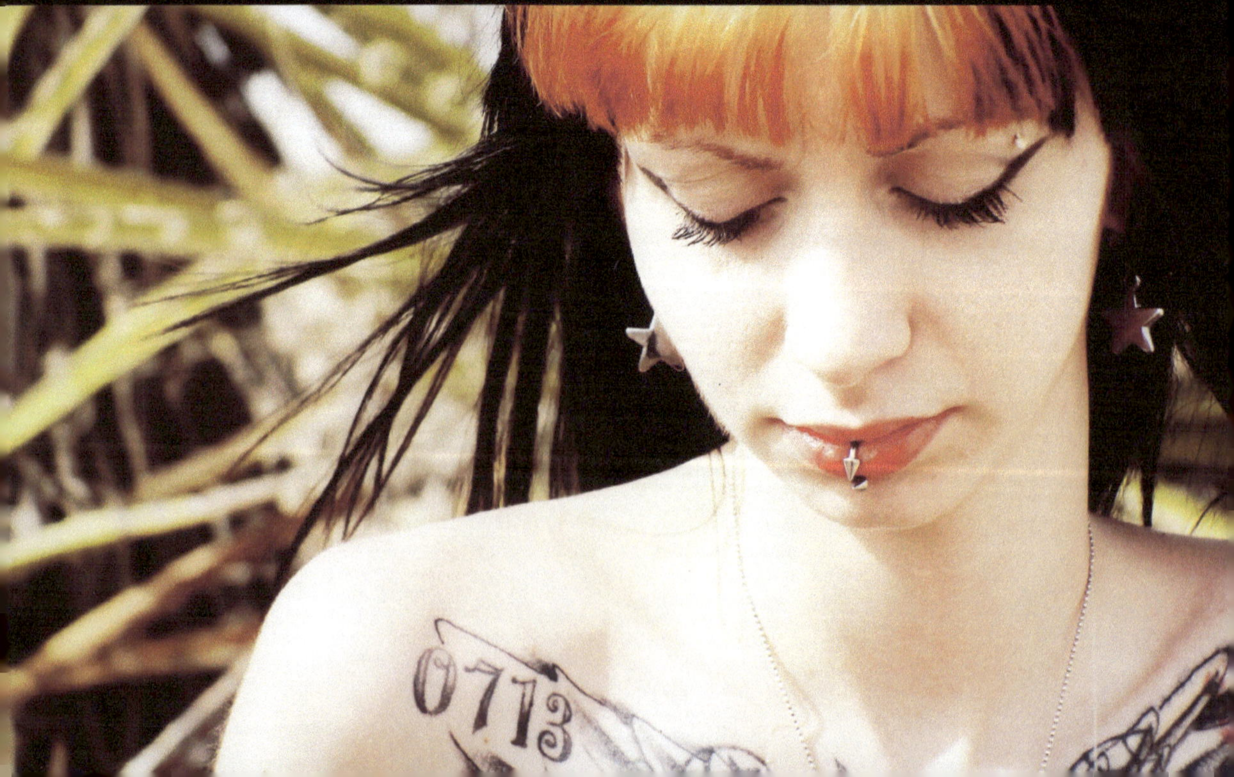
0713

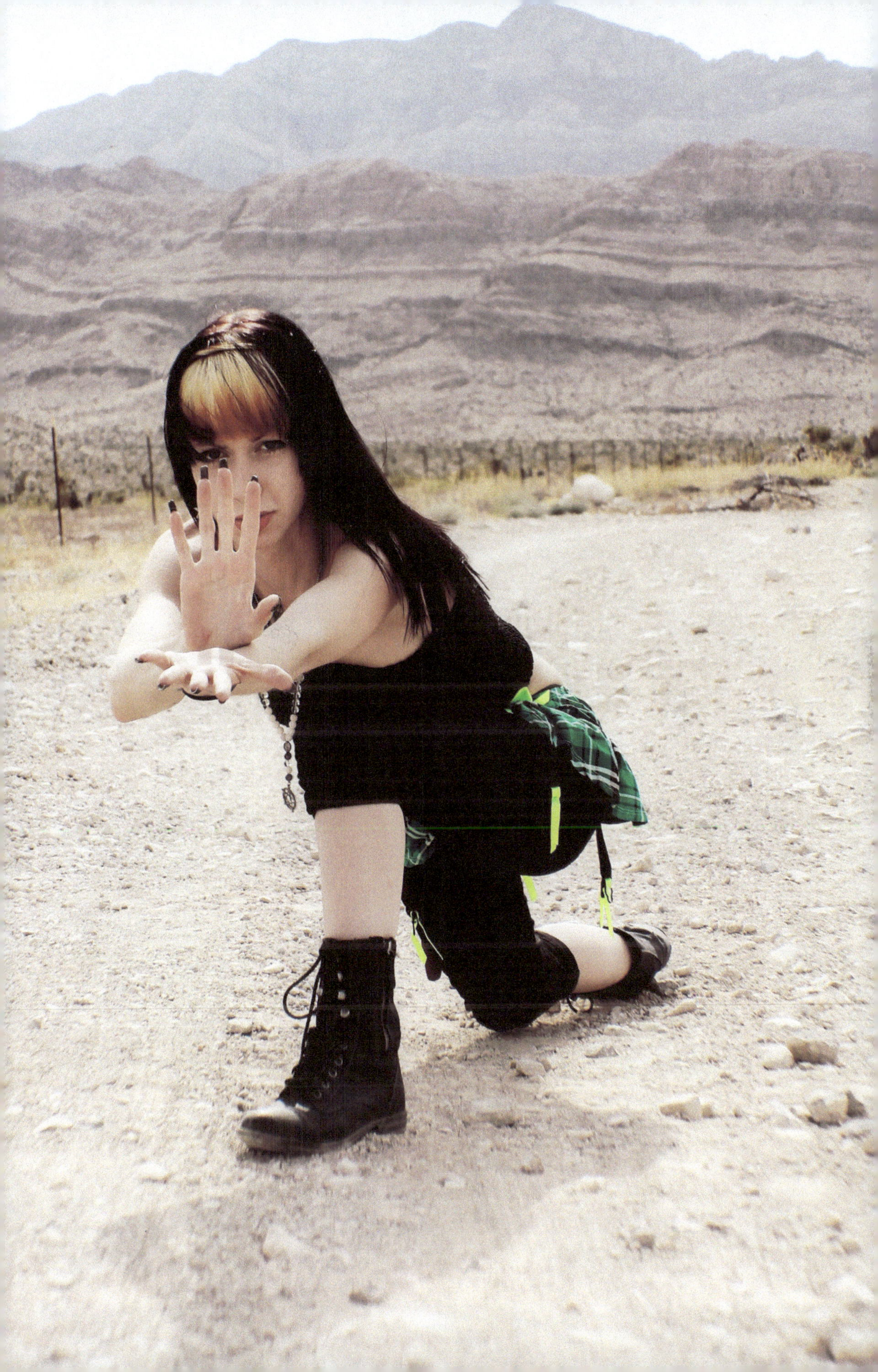

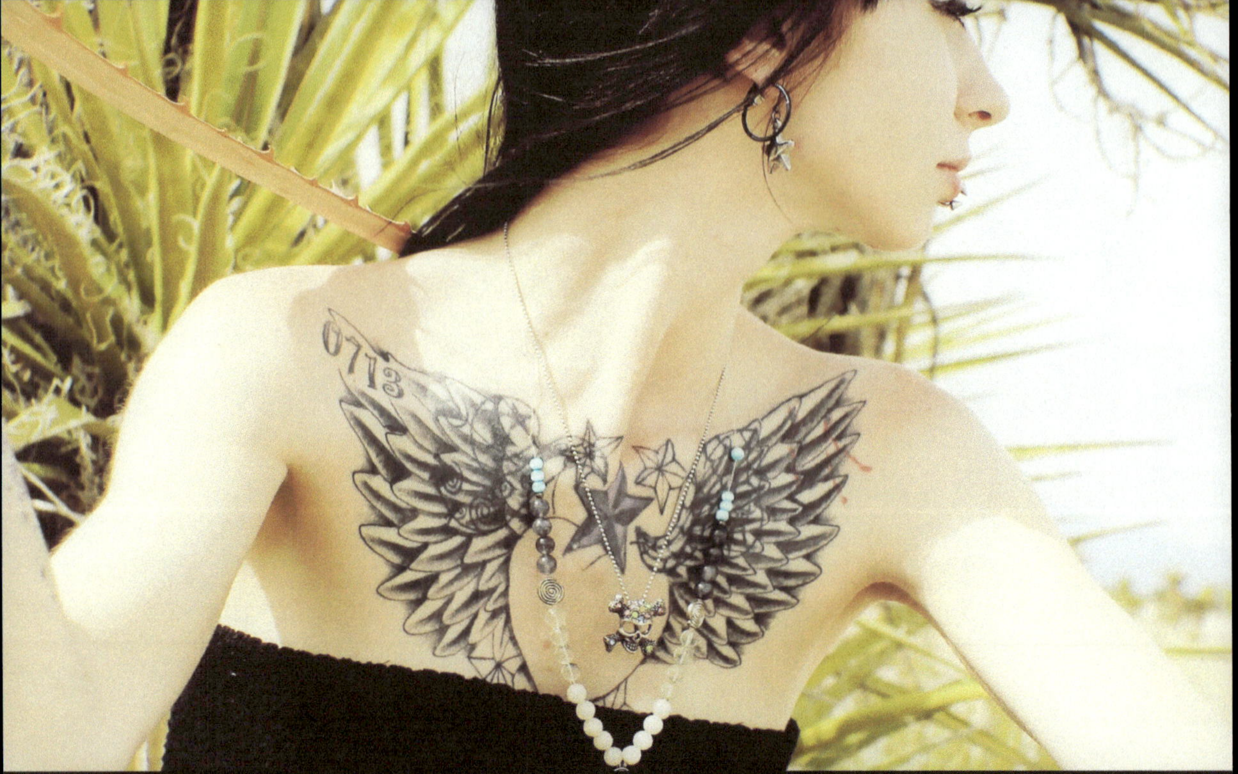
0713

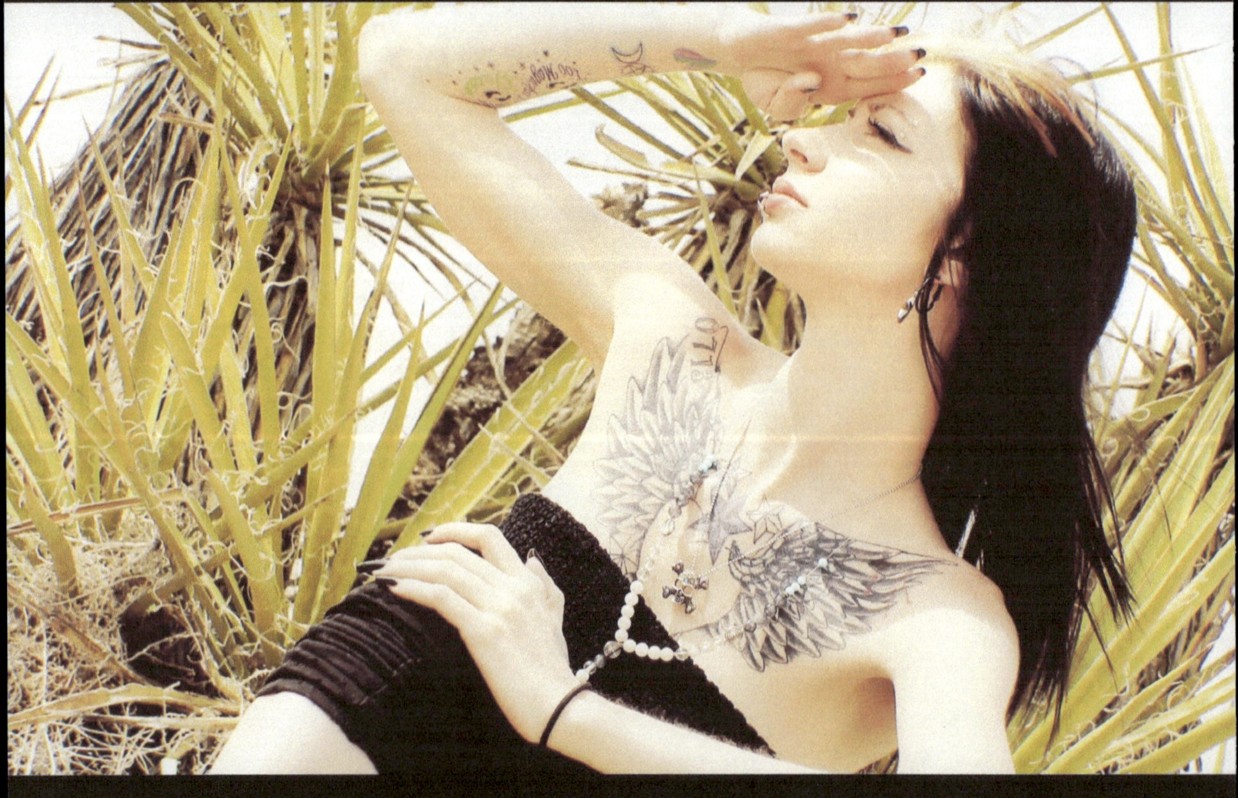

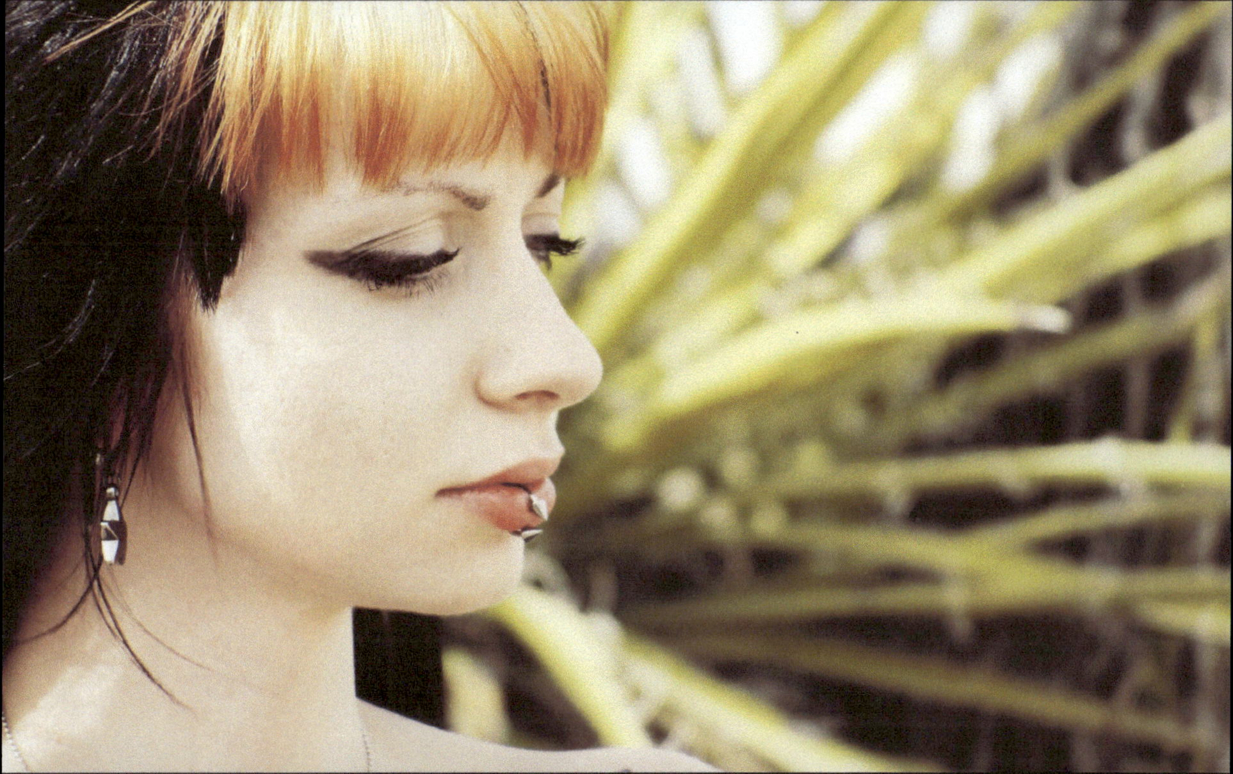

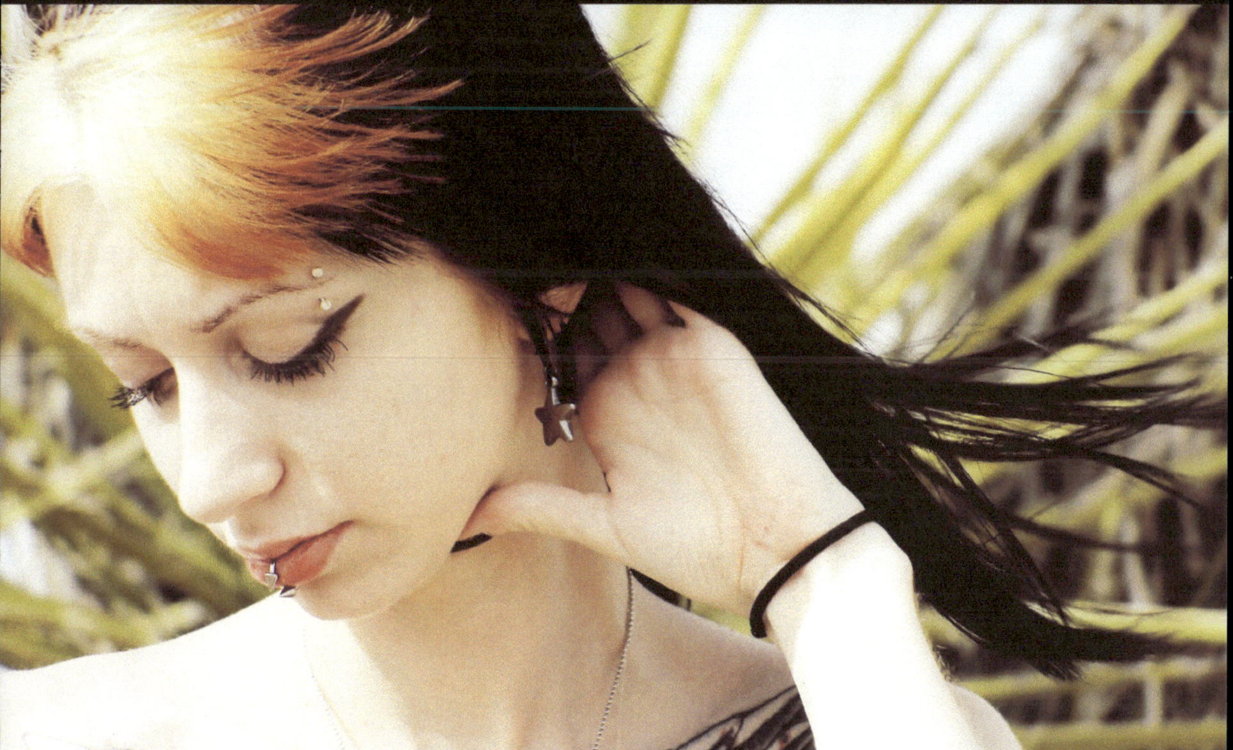

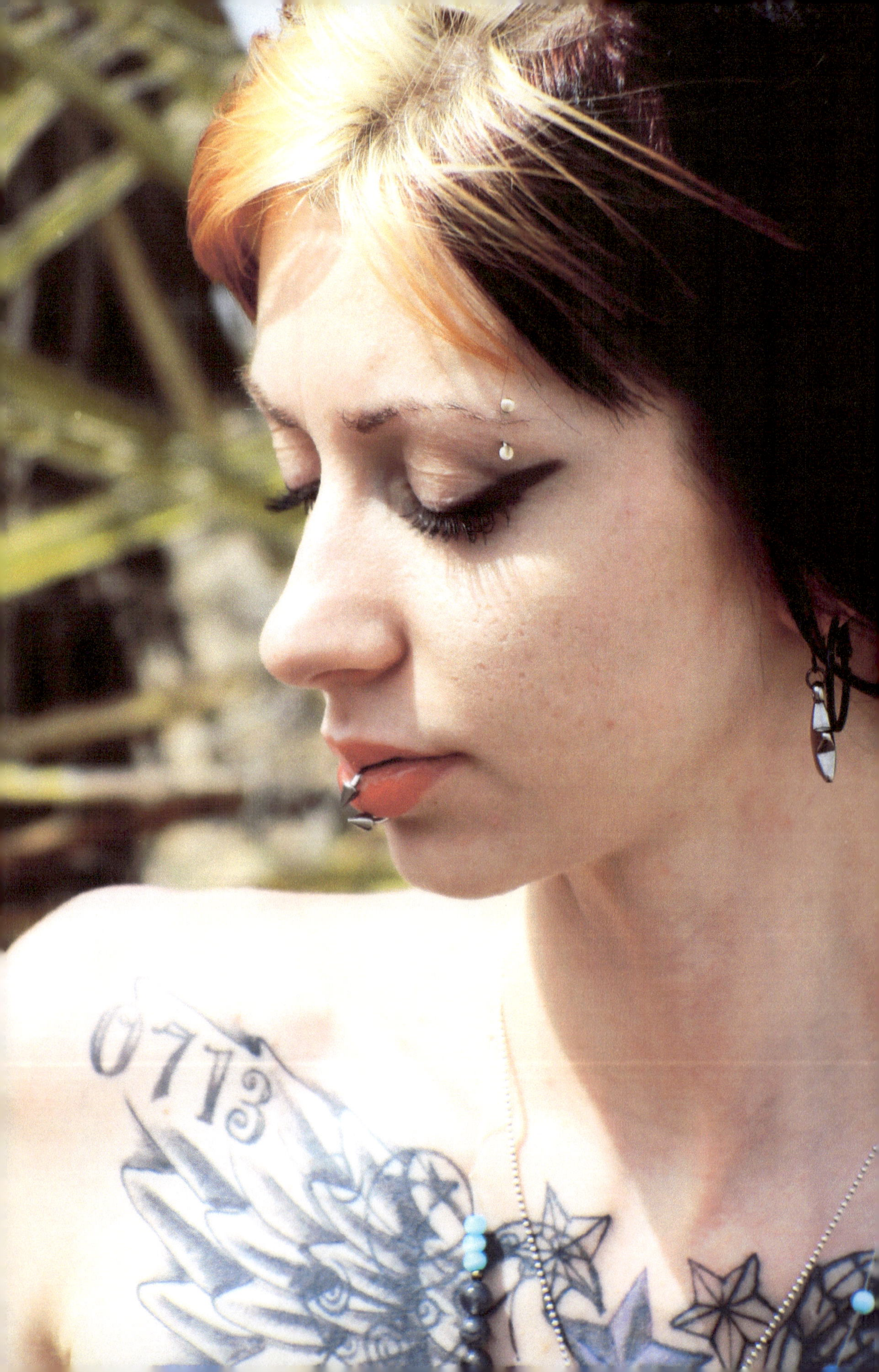
0713

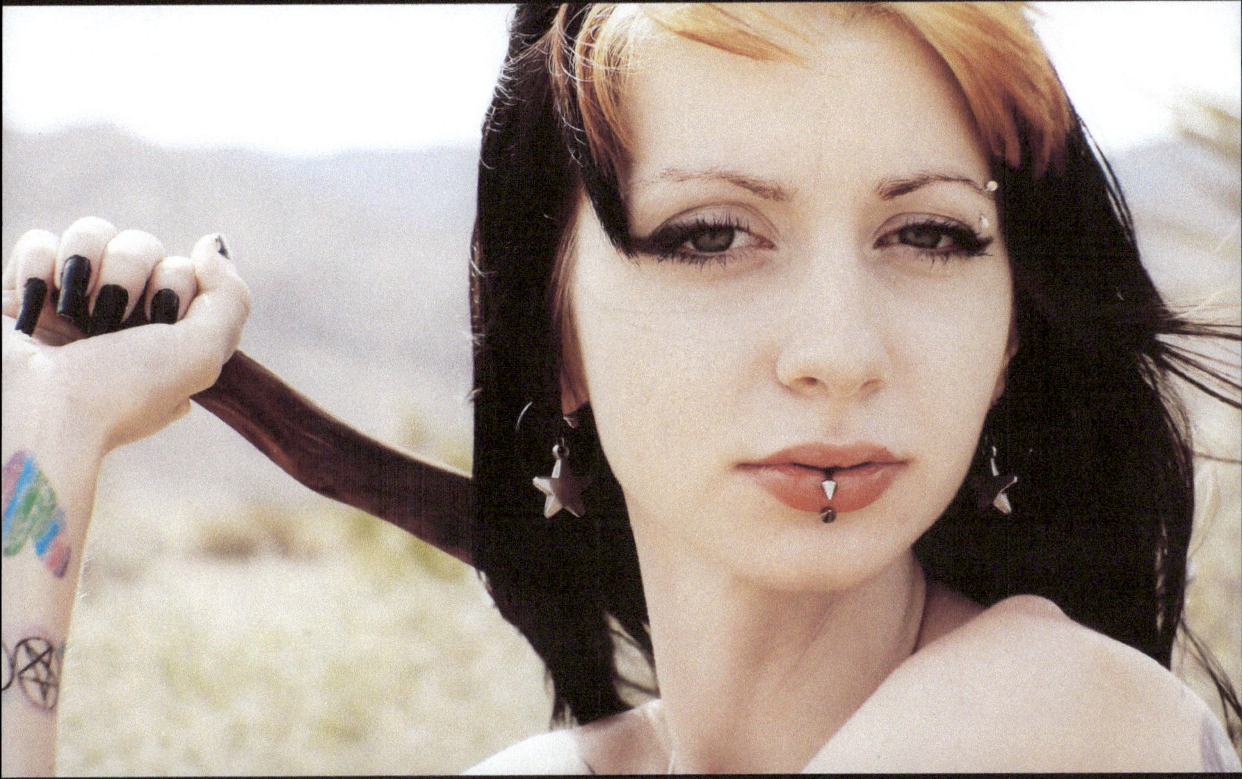

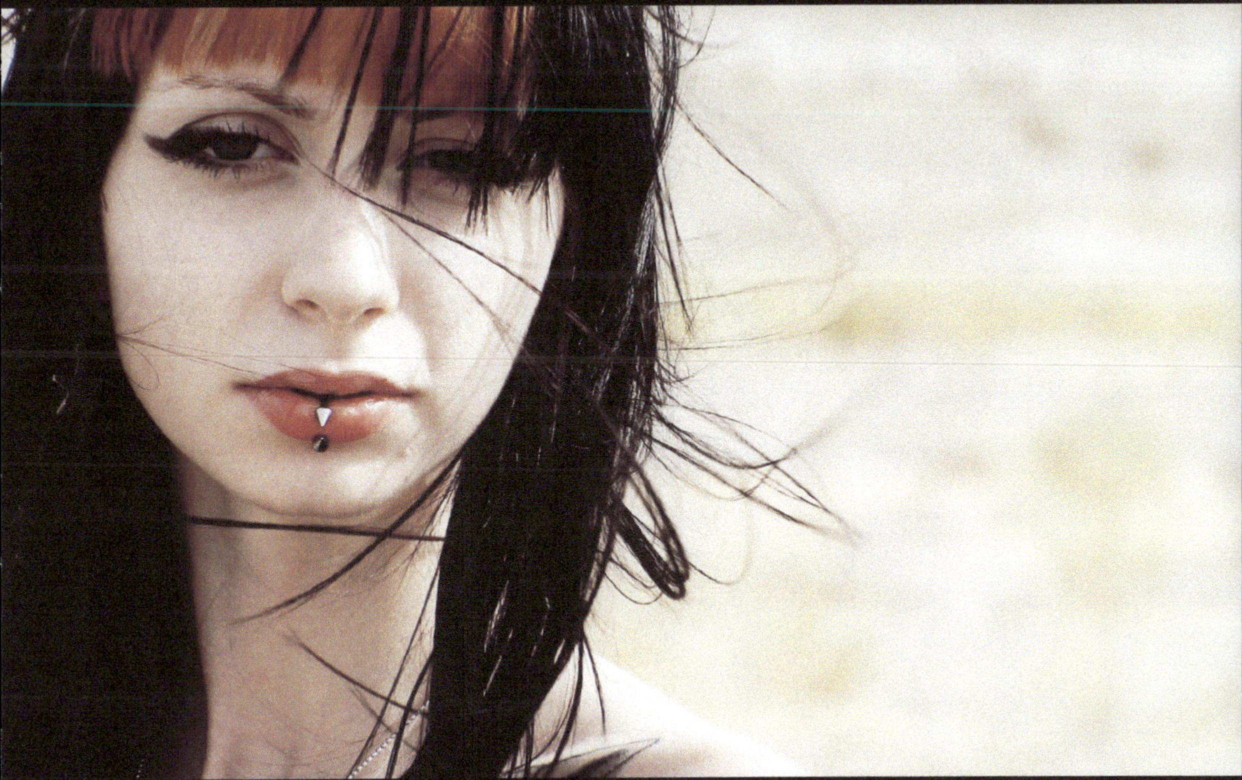

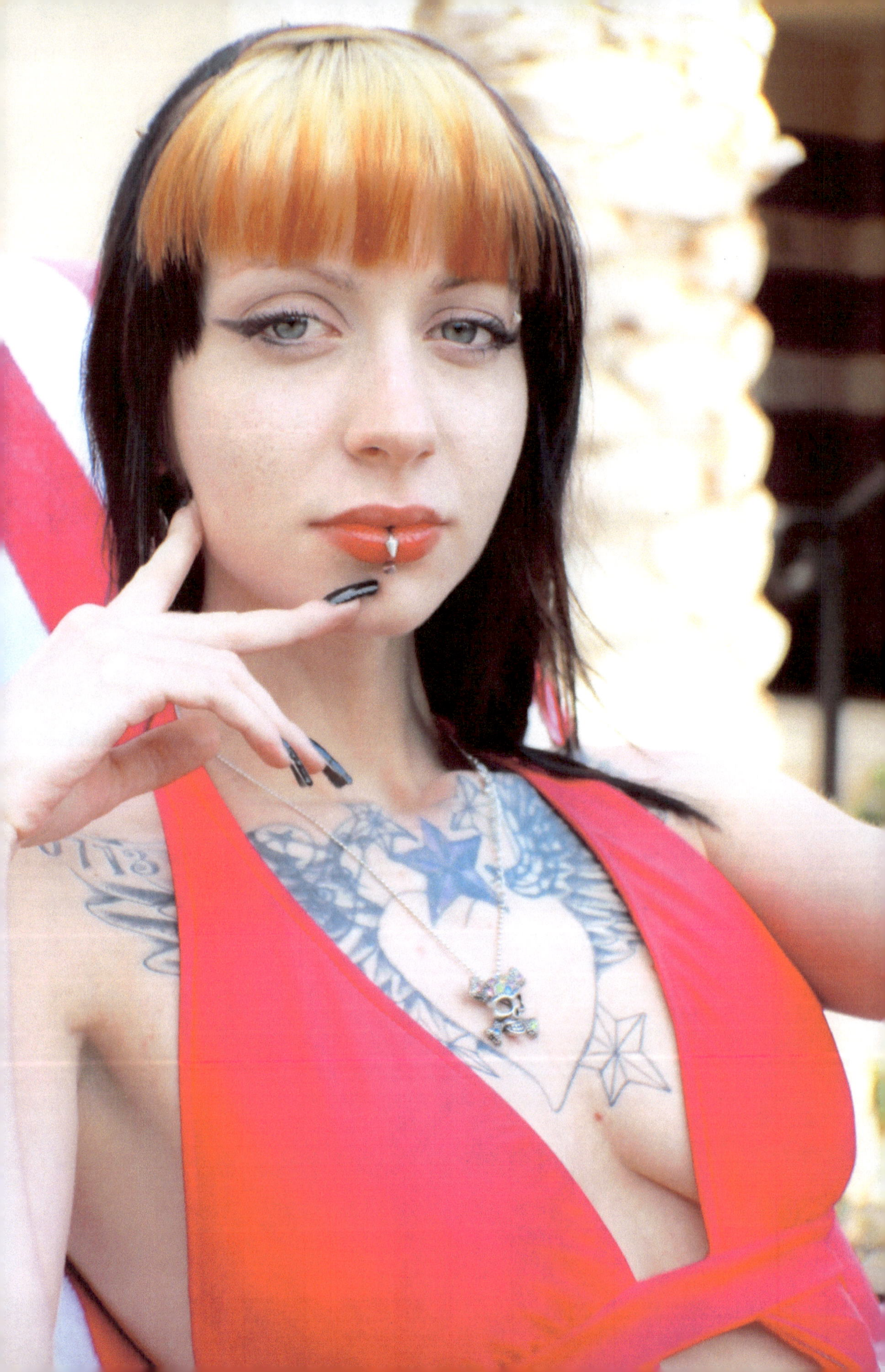

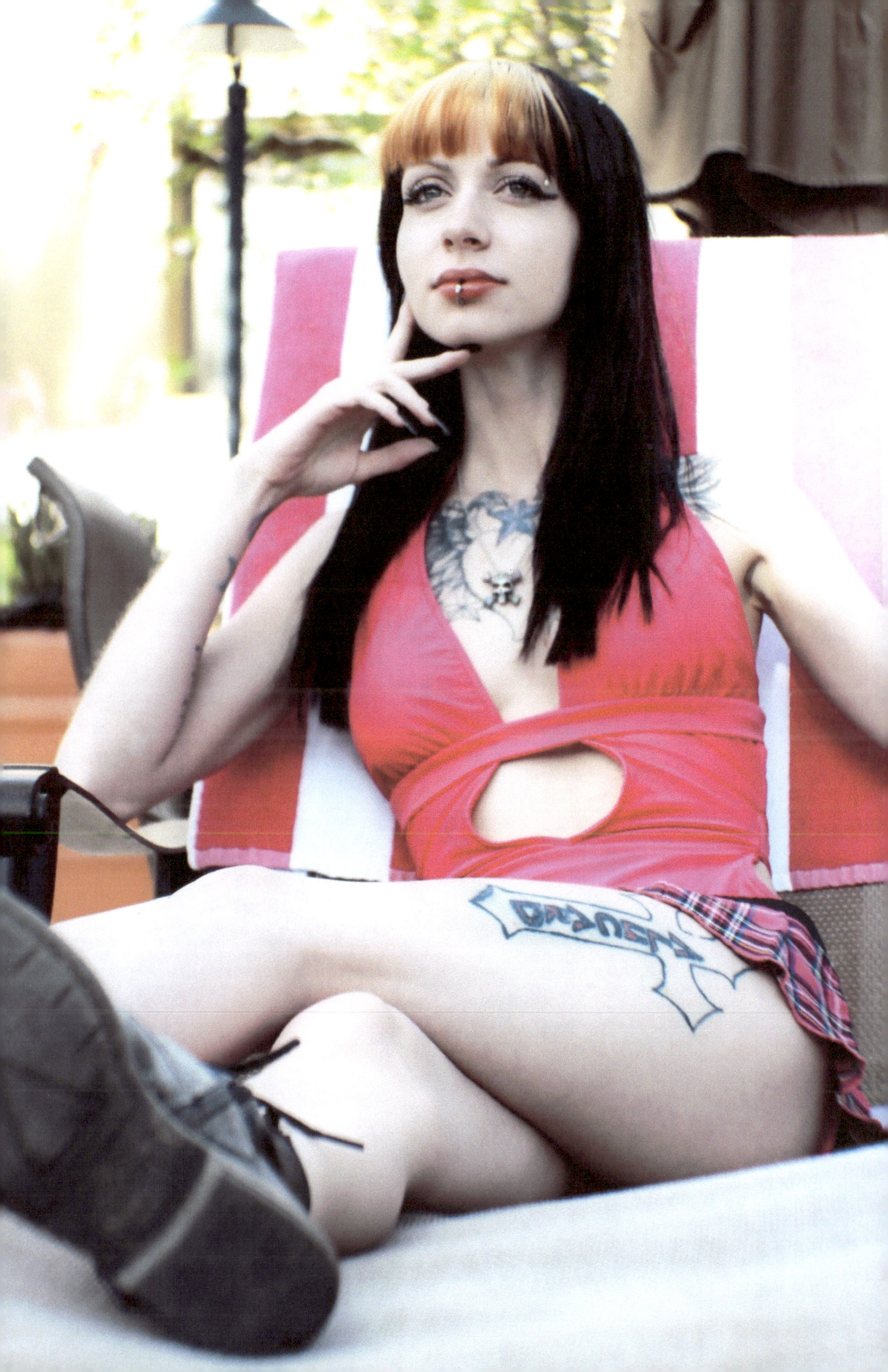

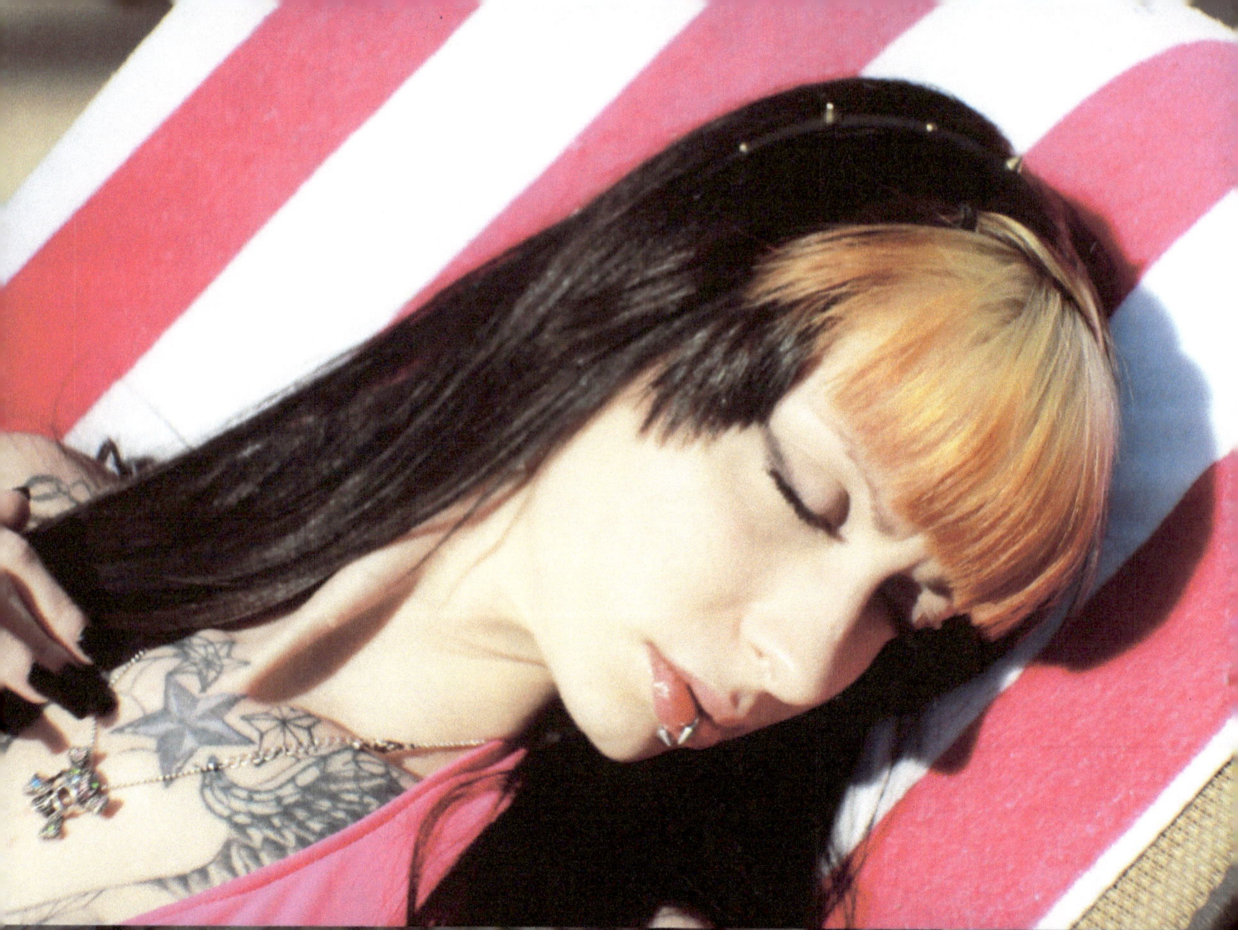

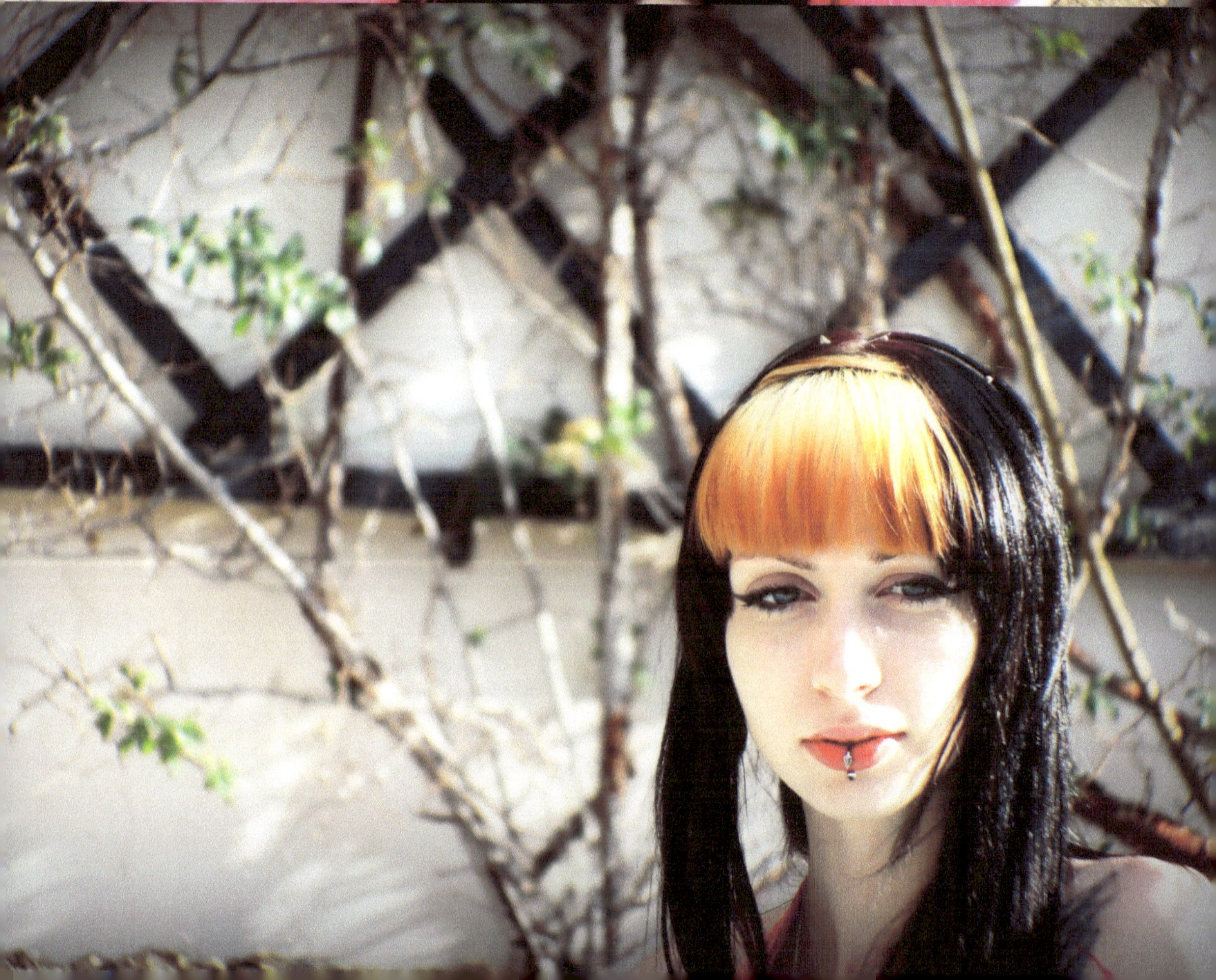

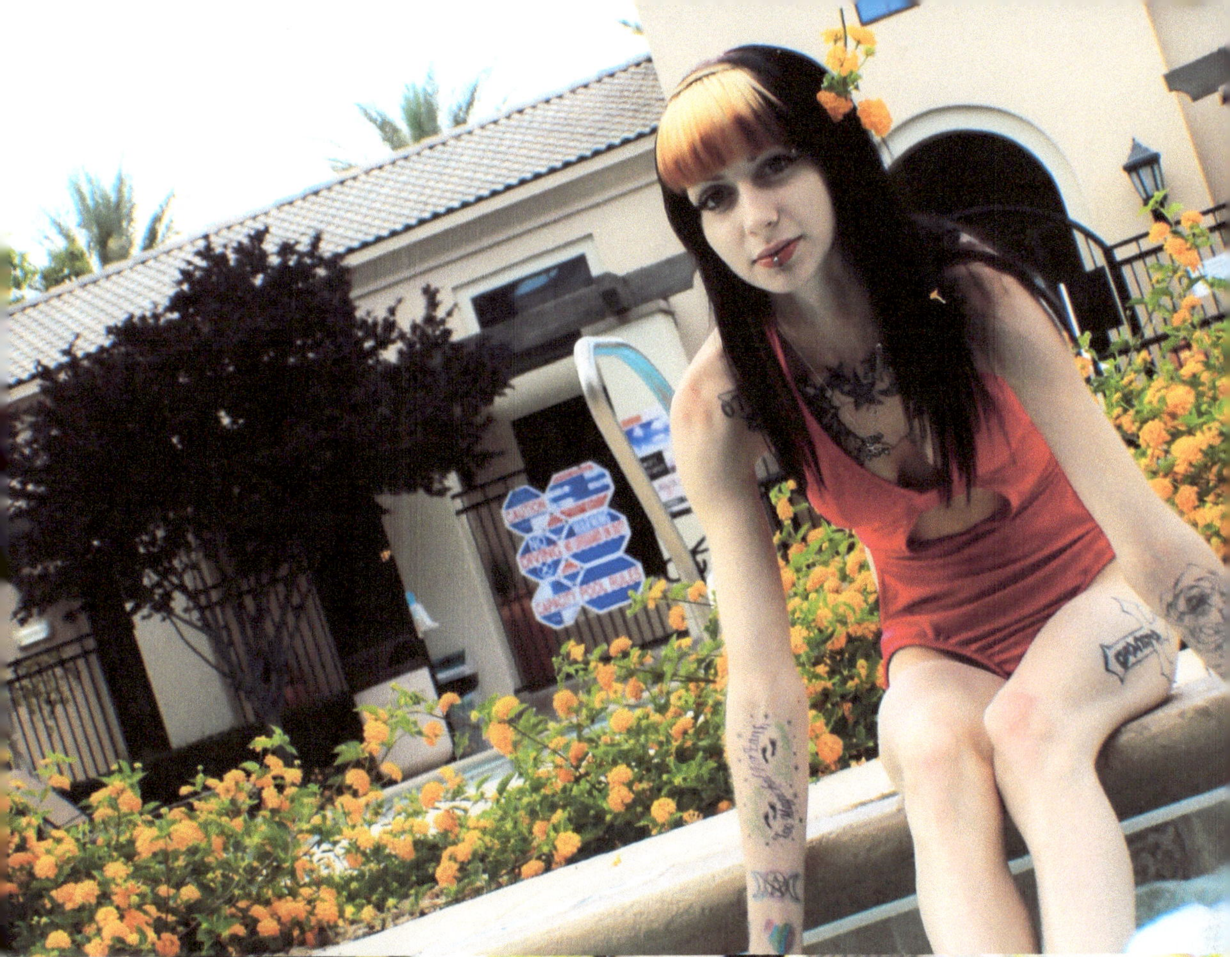

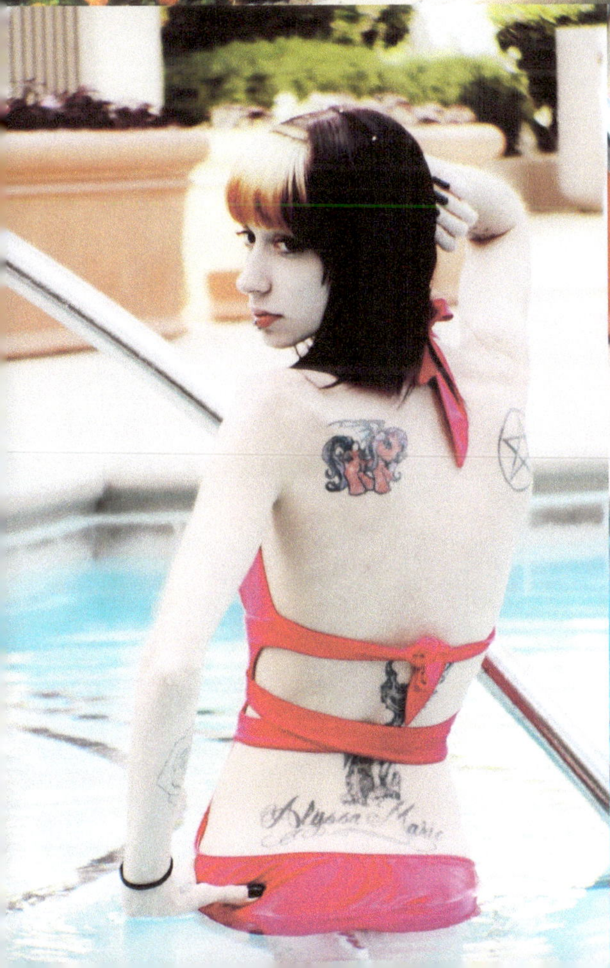

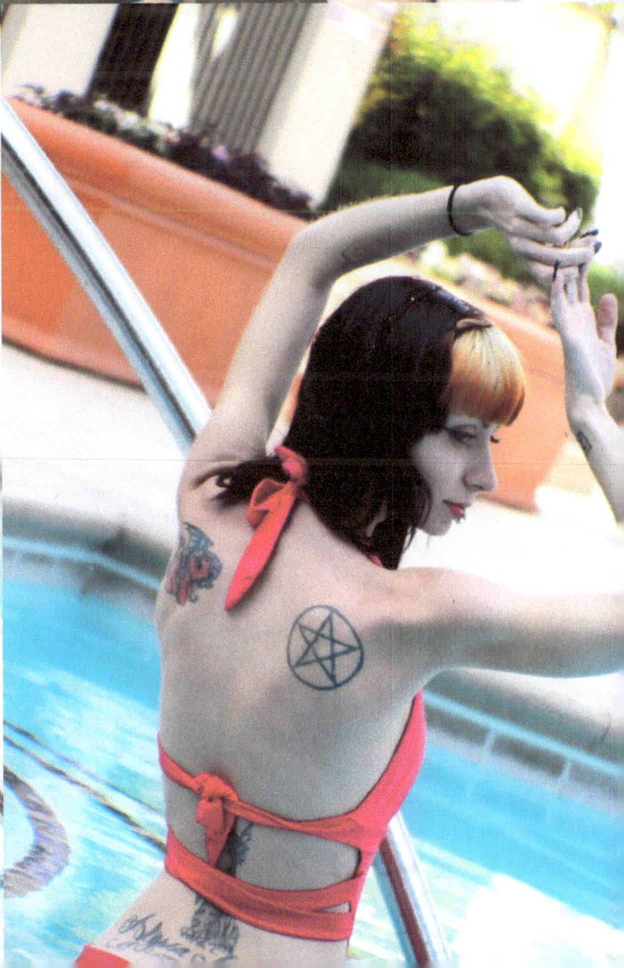

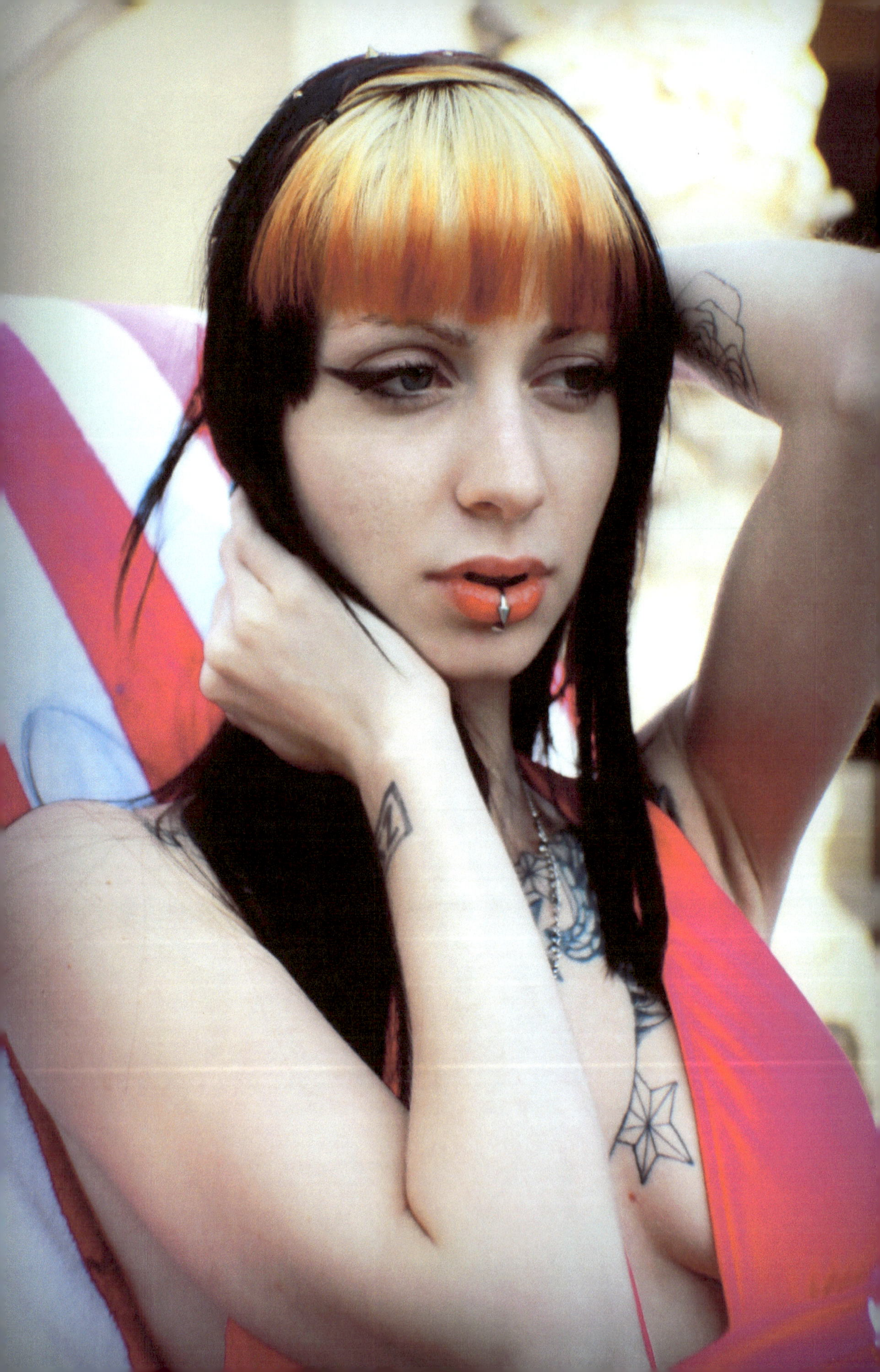

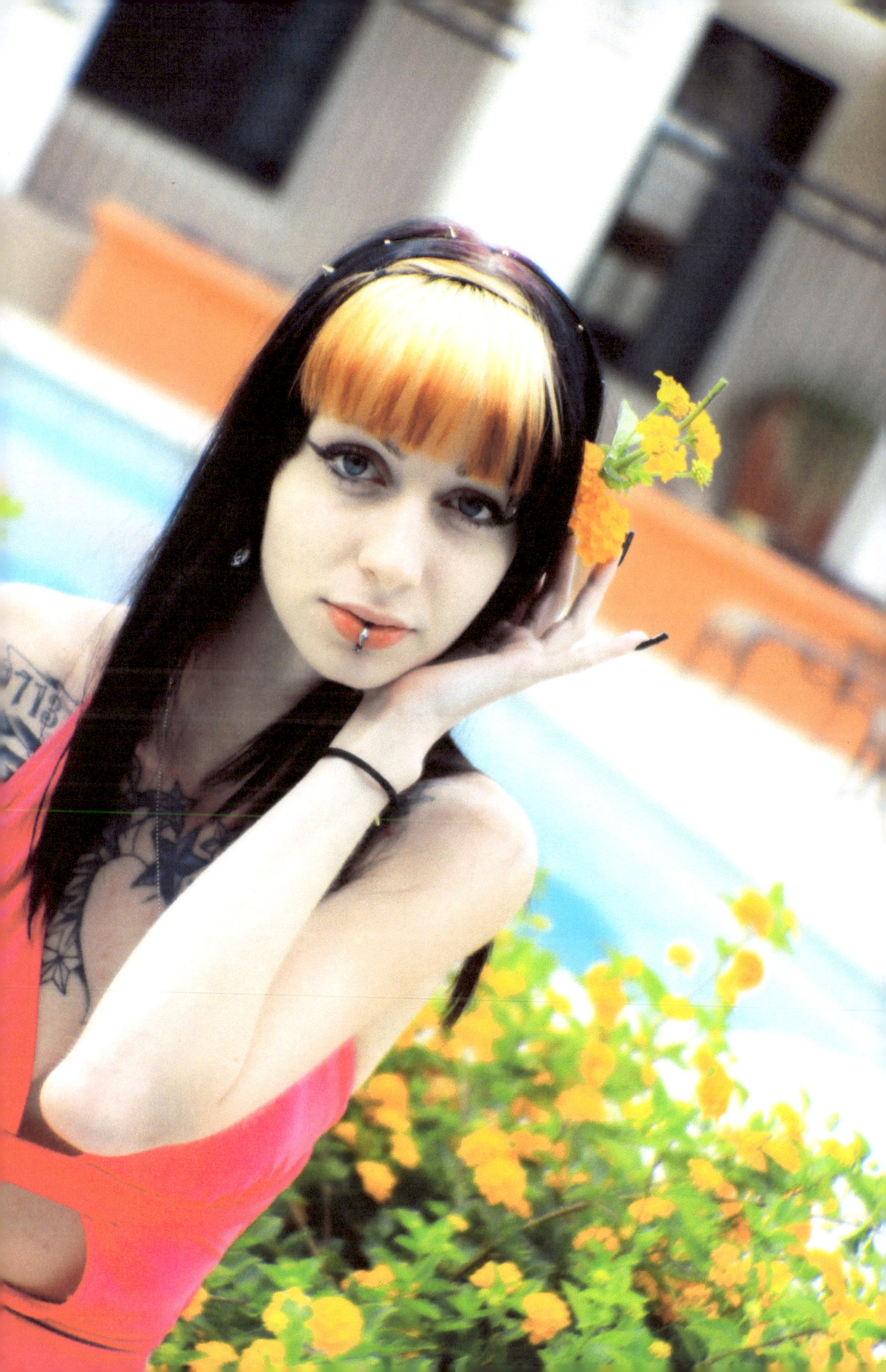

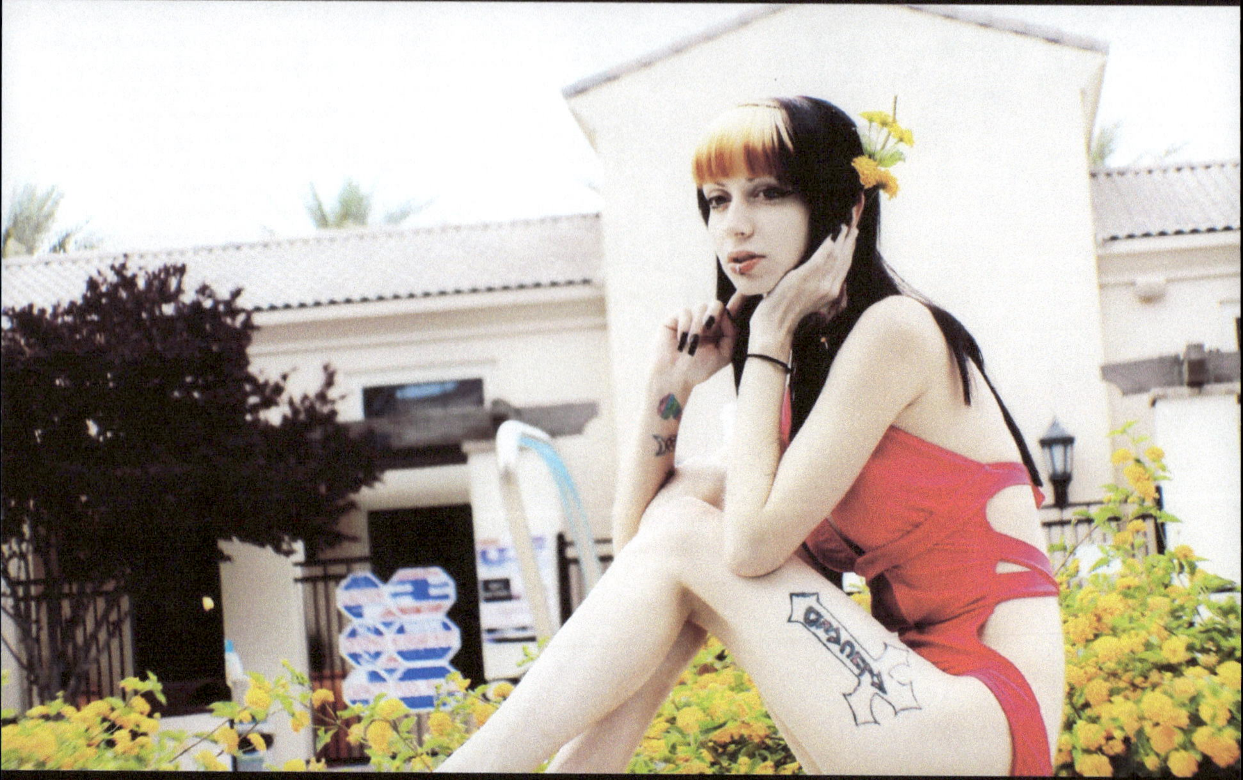

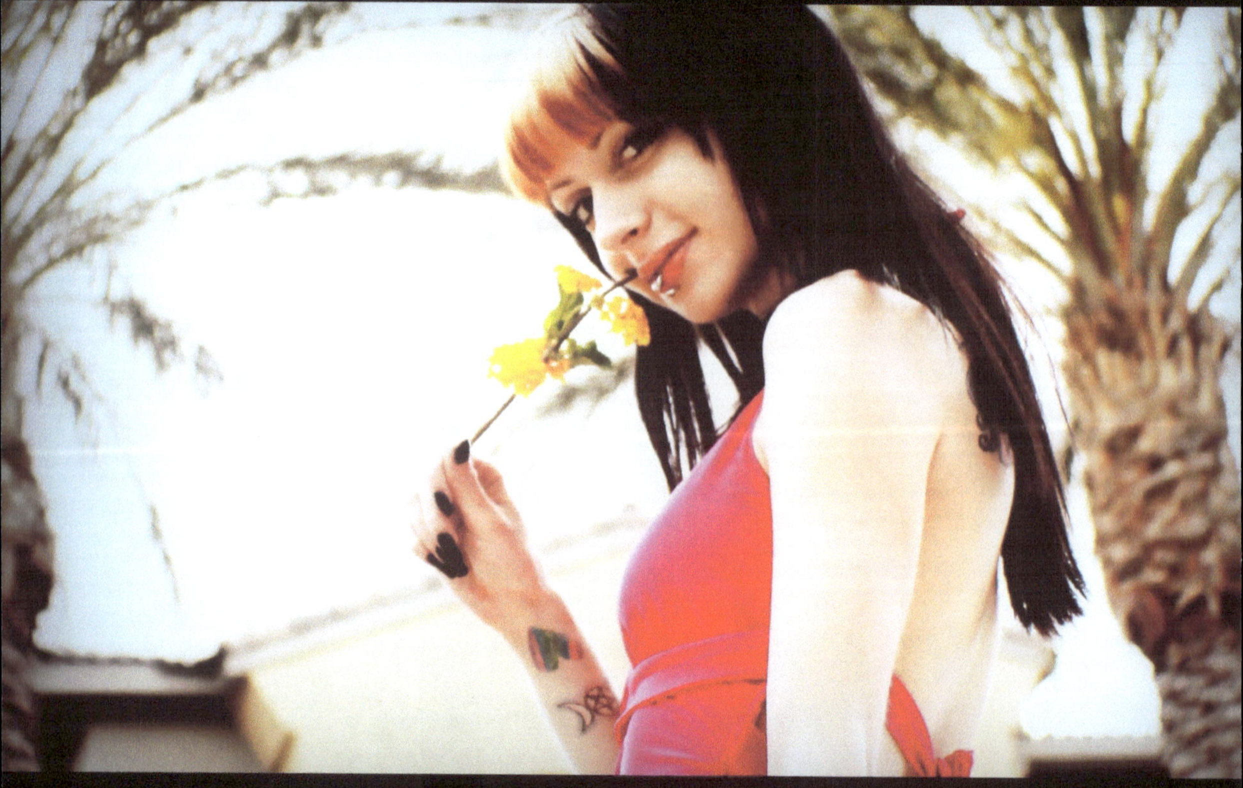

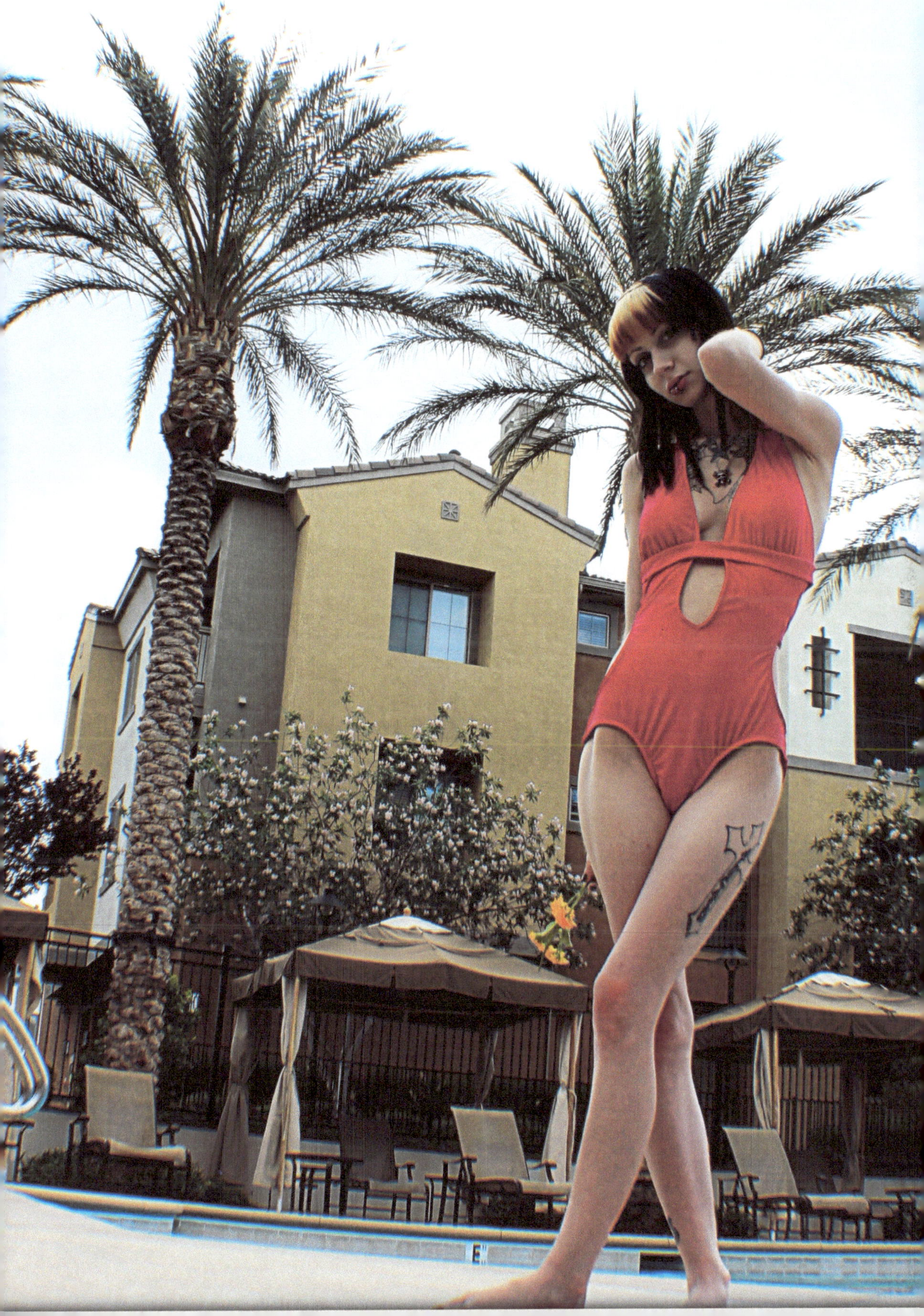

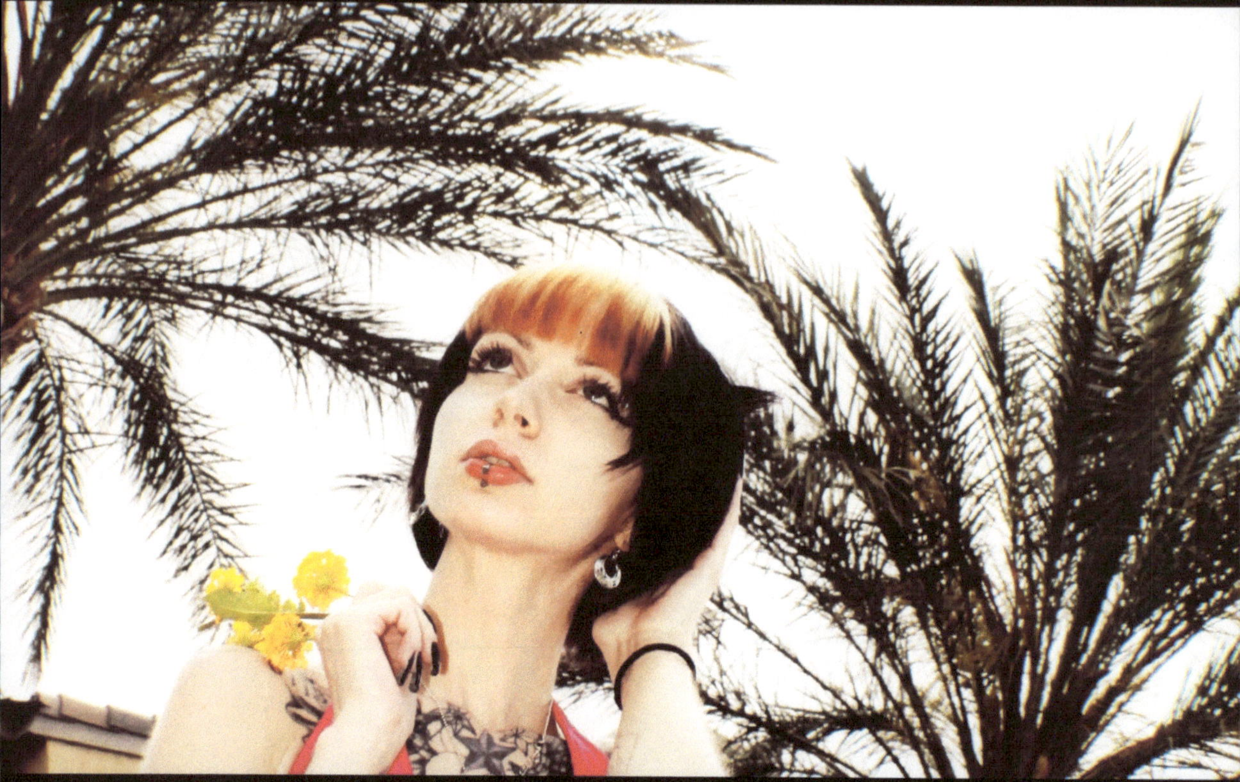

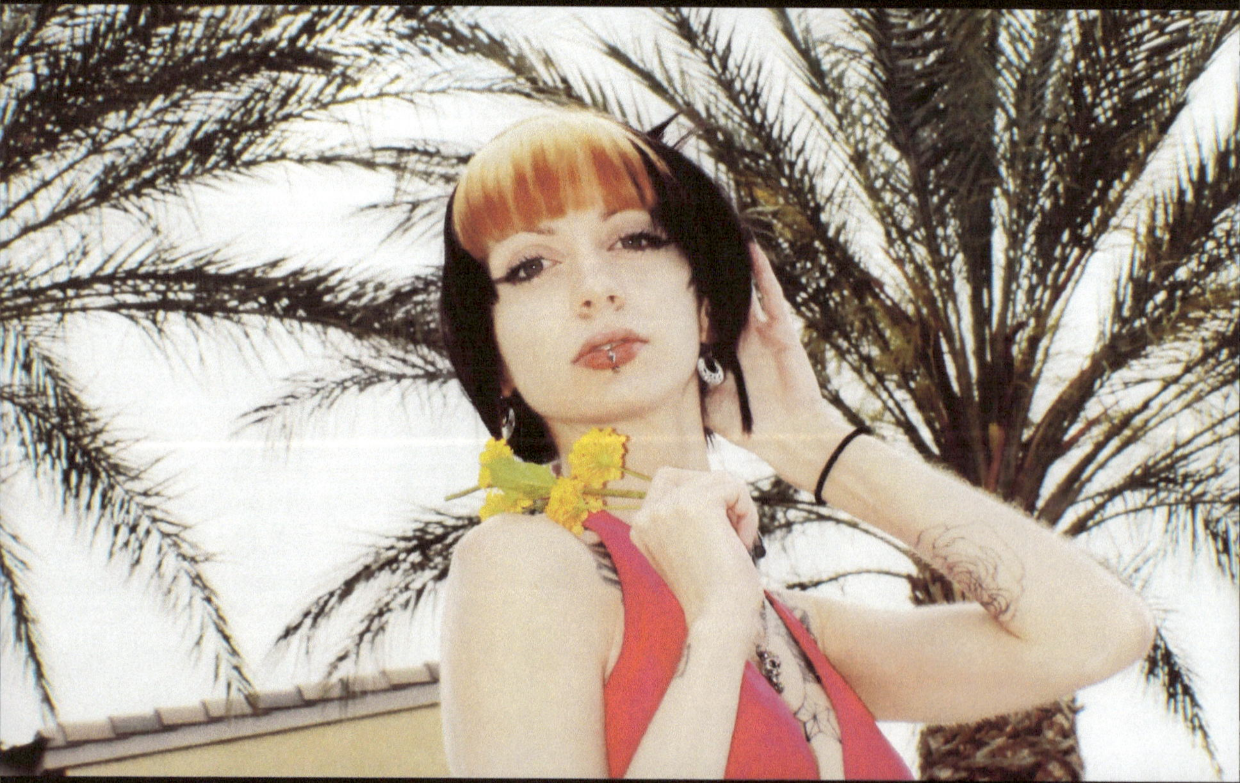

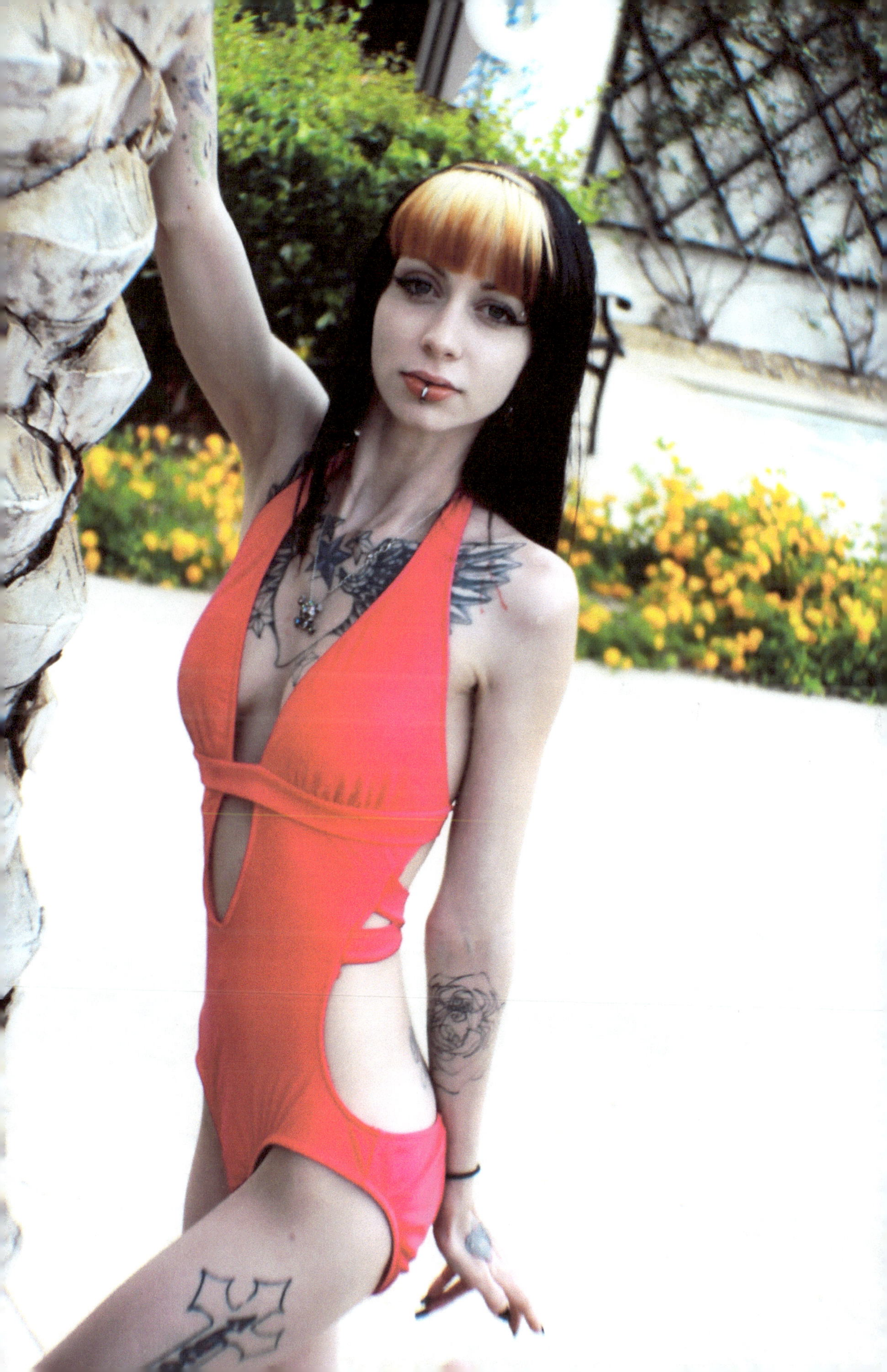

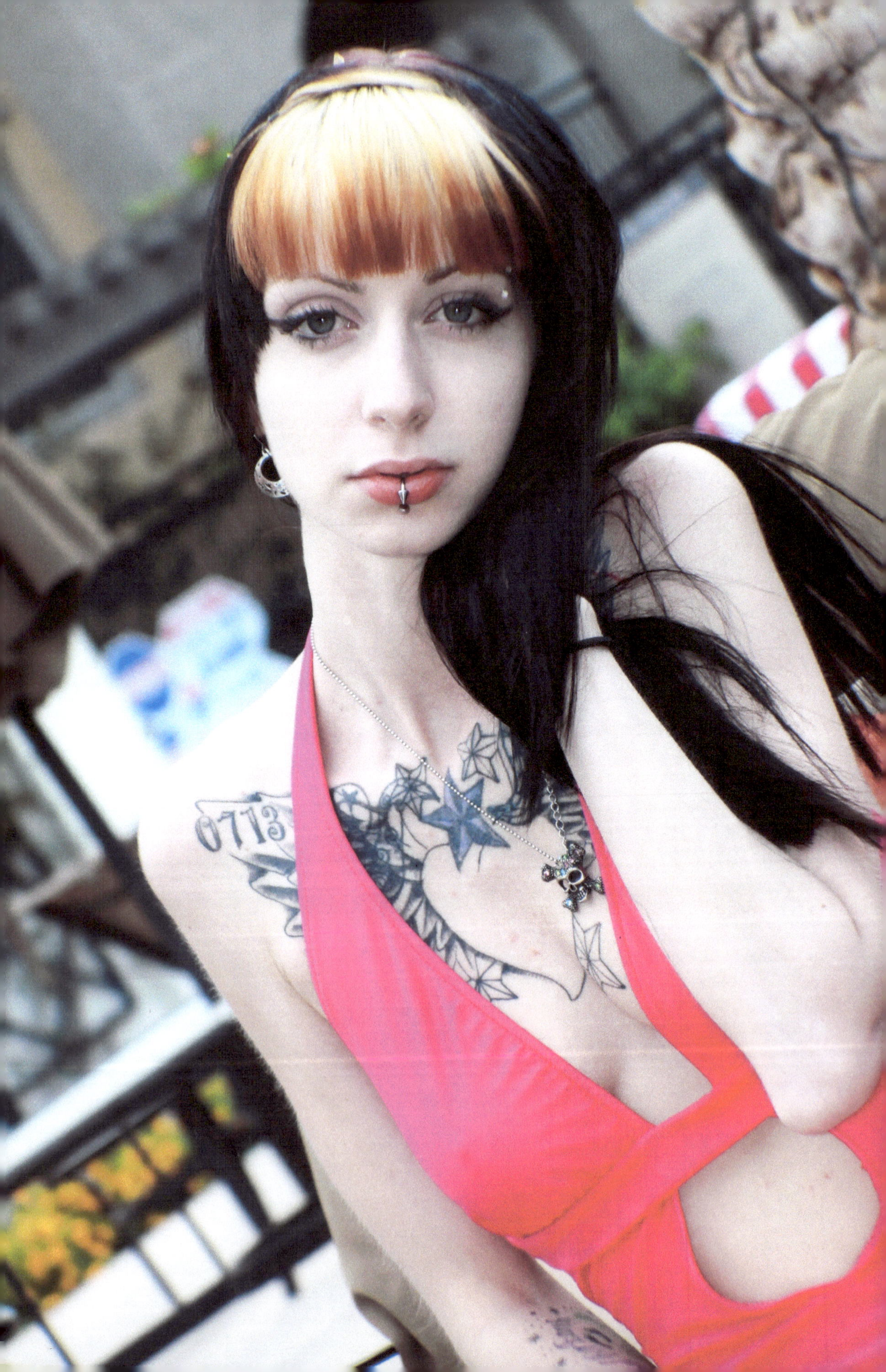
0713

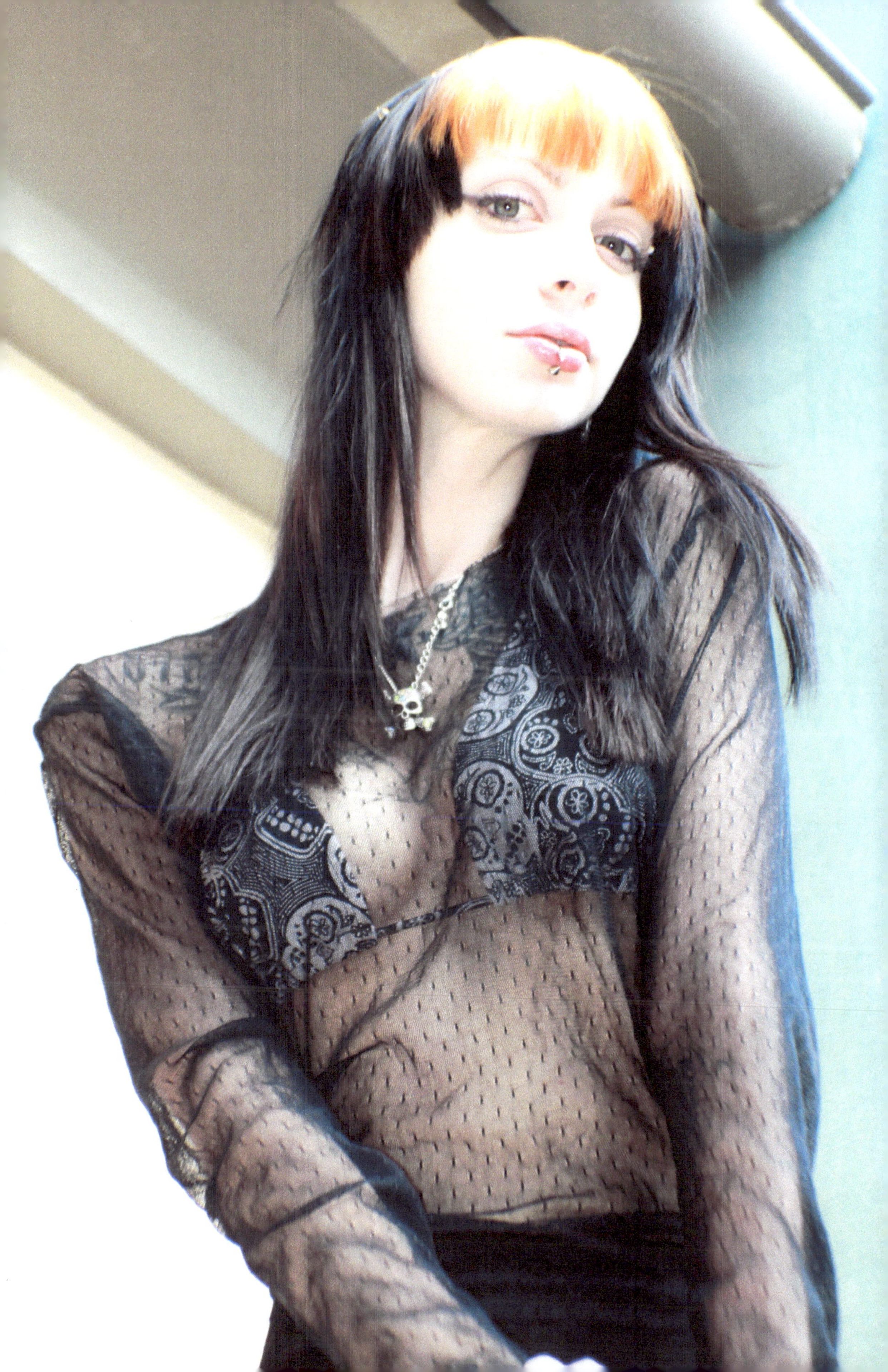

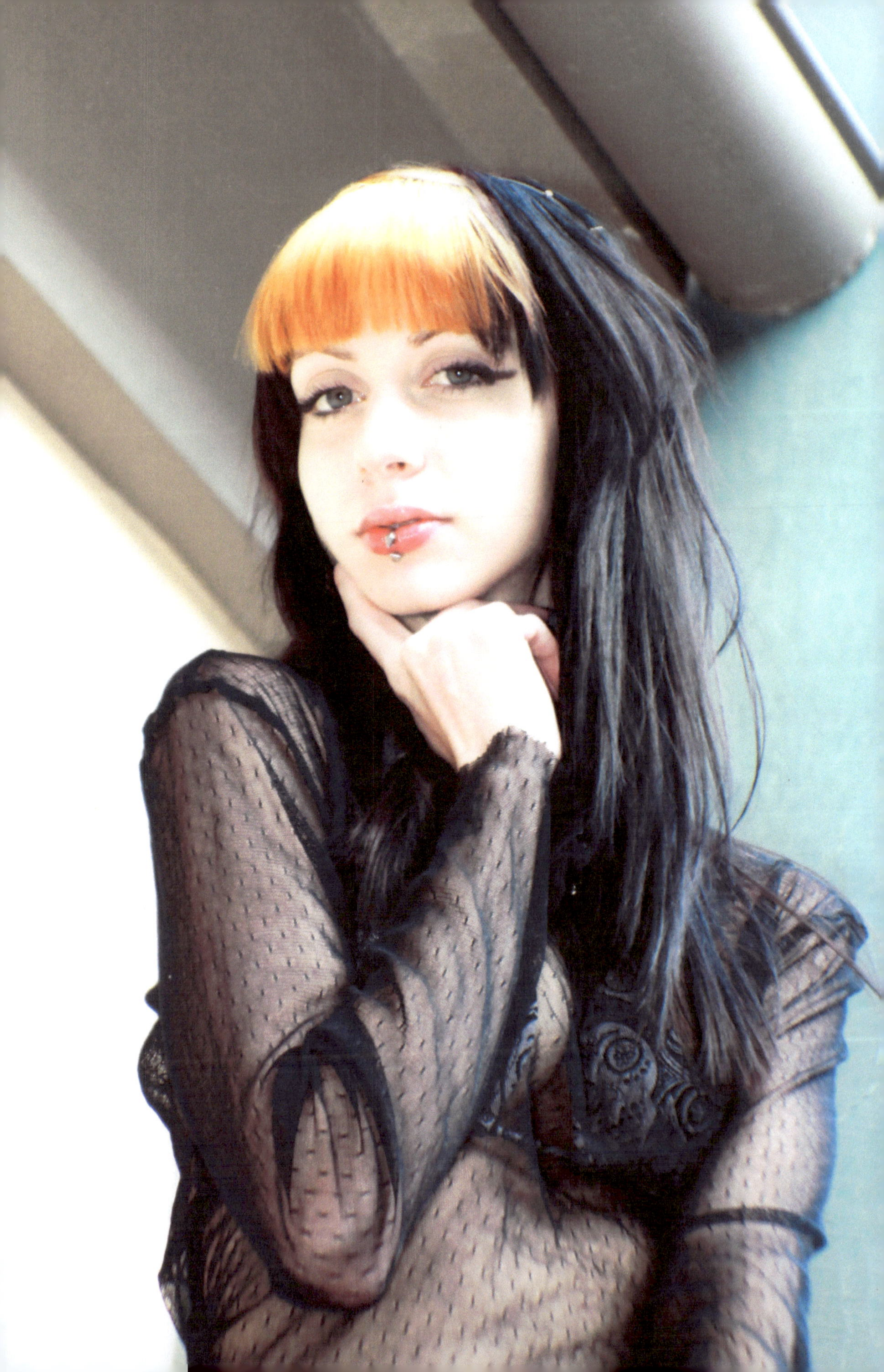

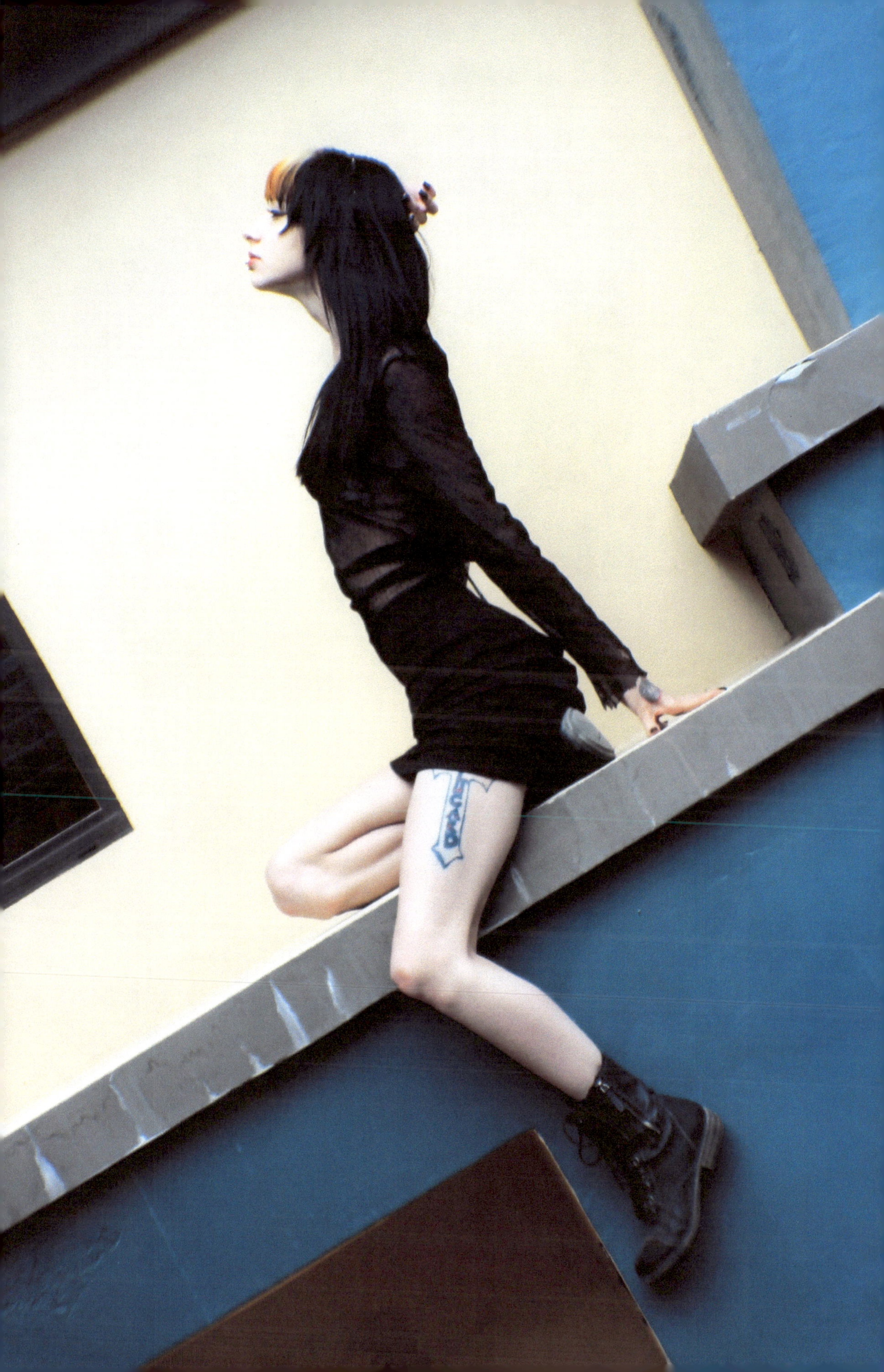

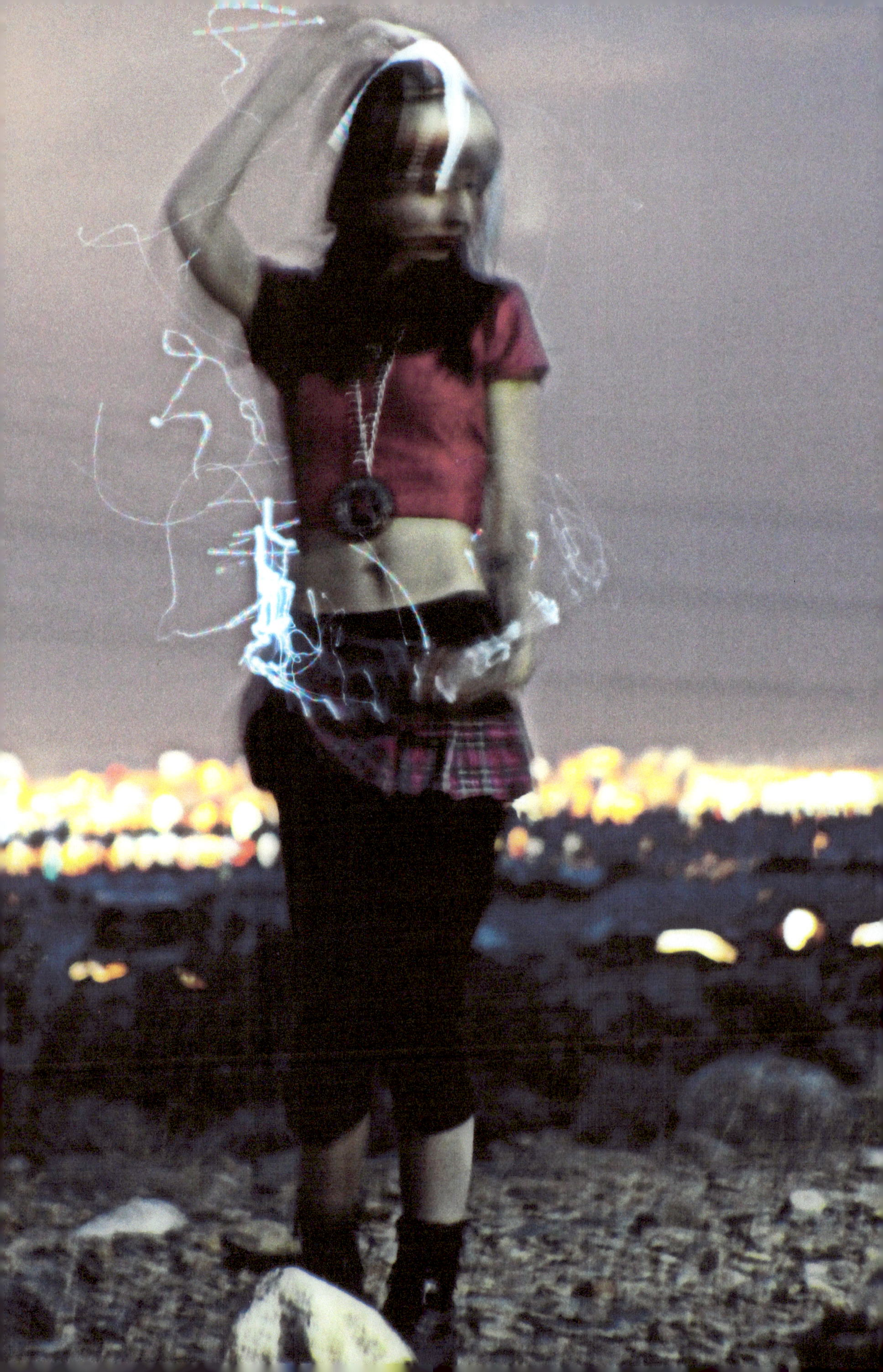

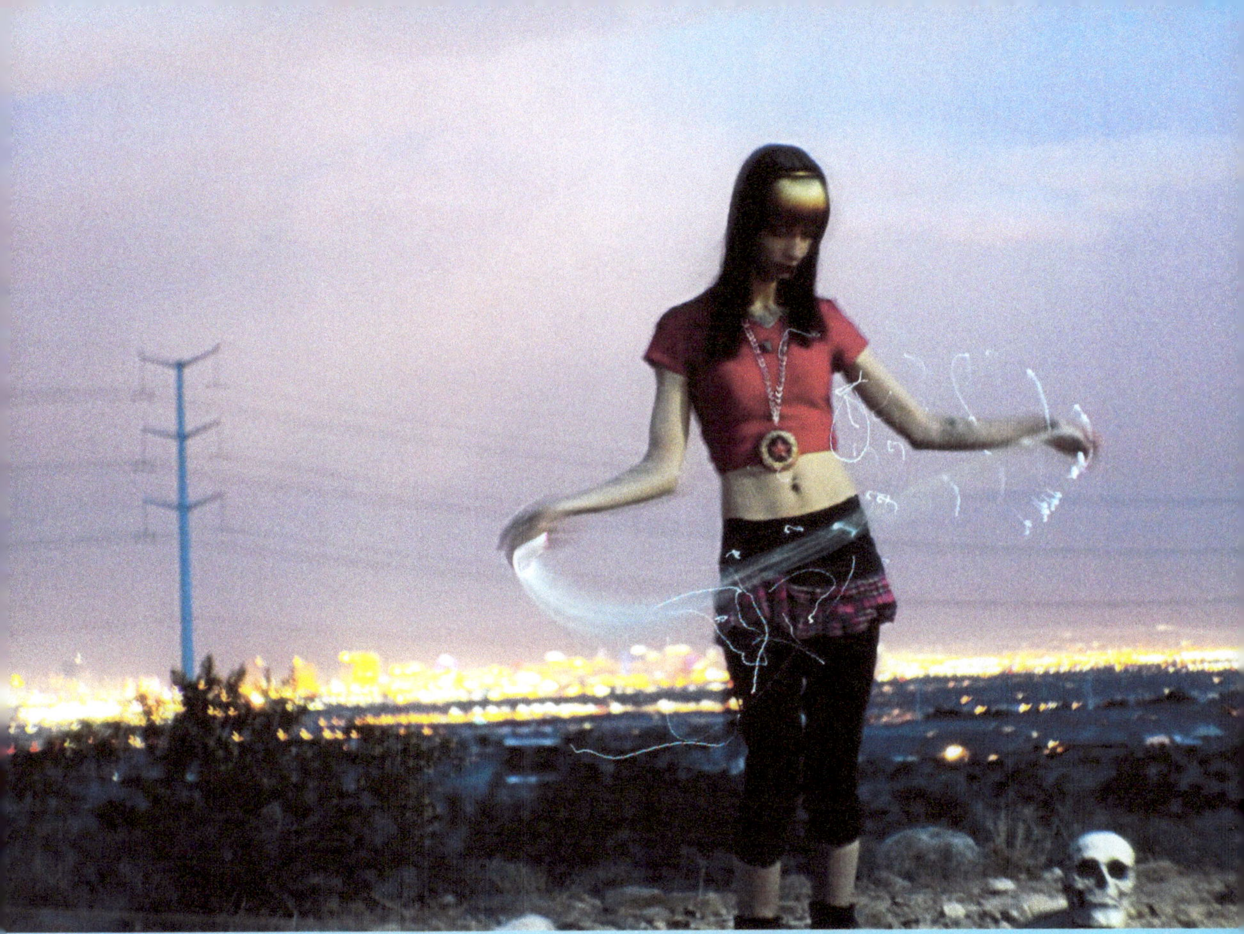

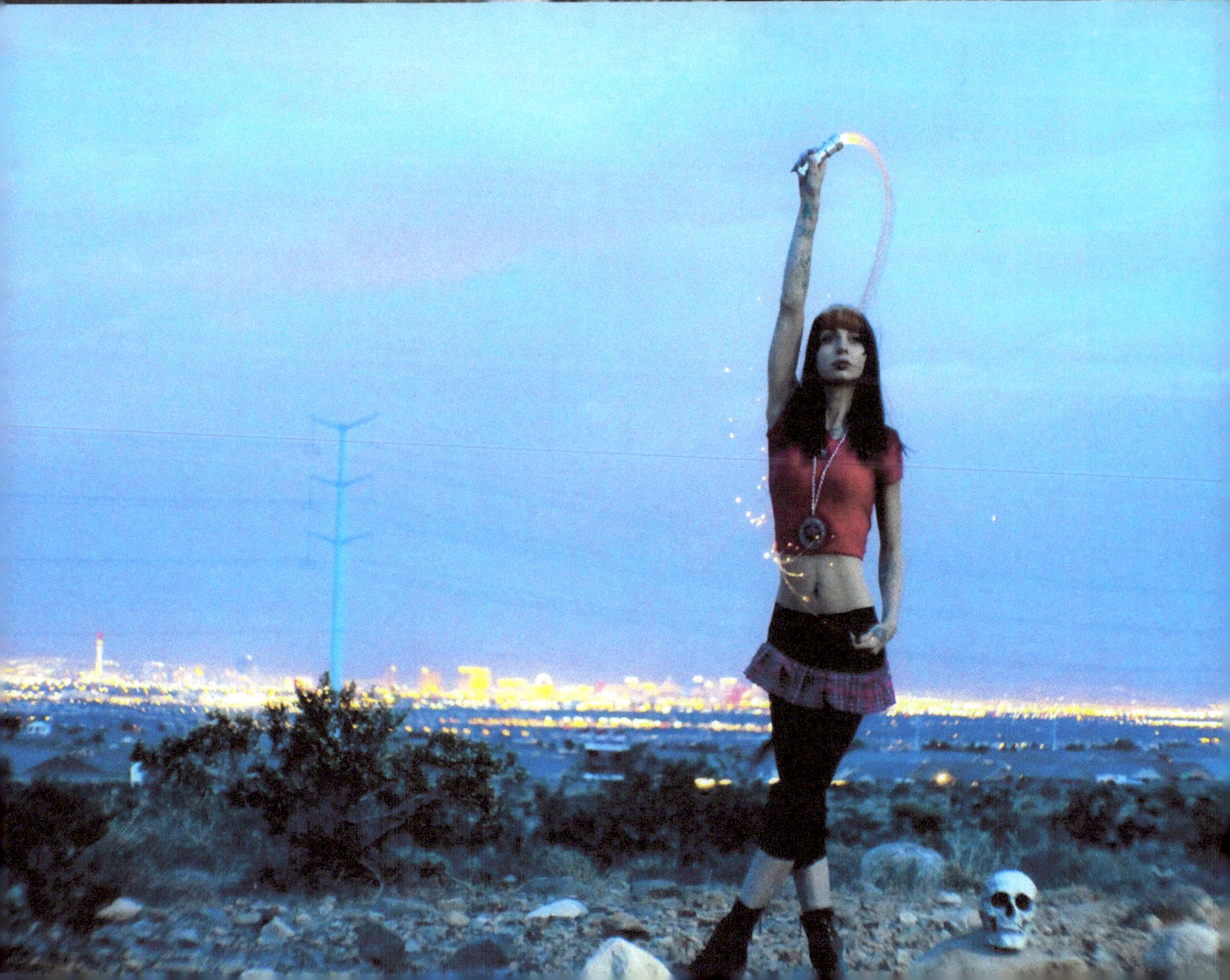

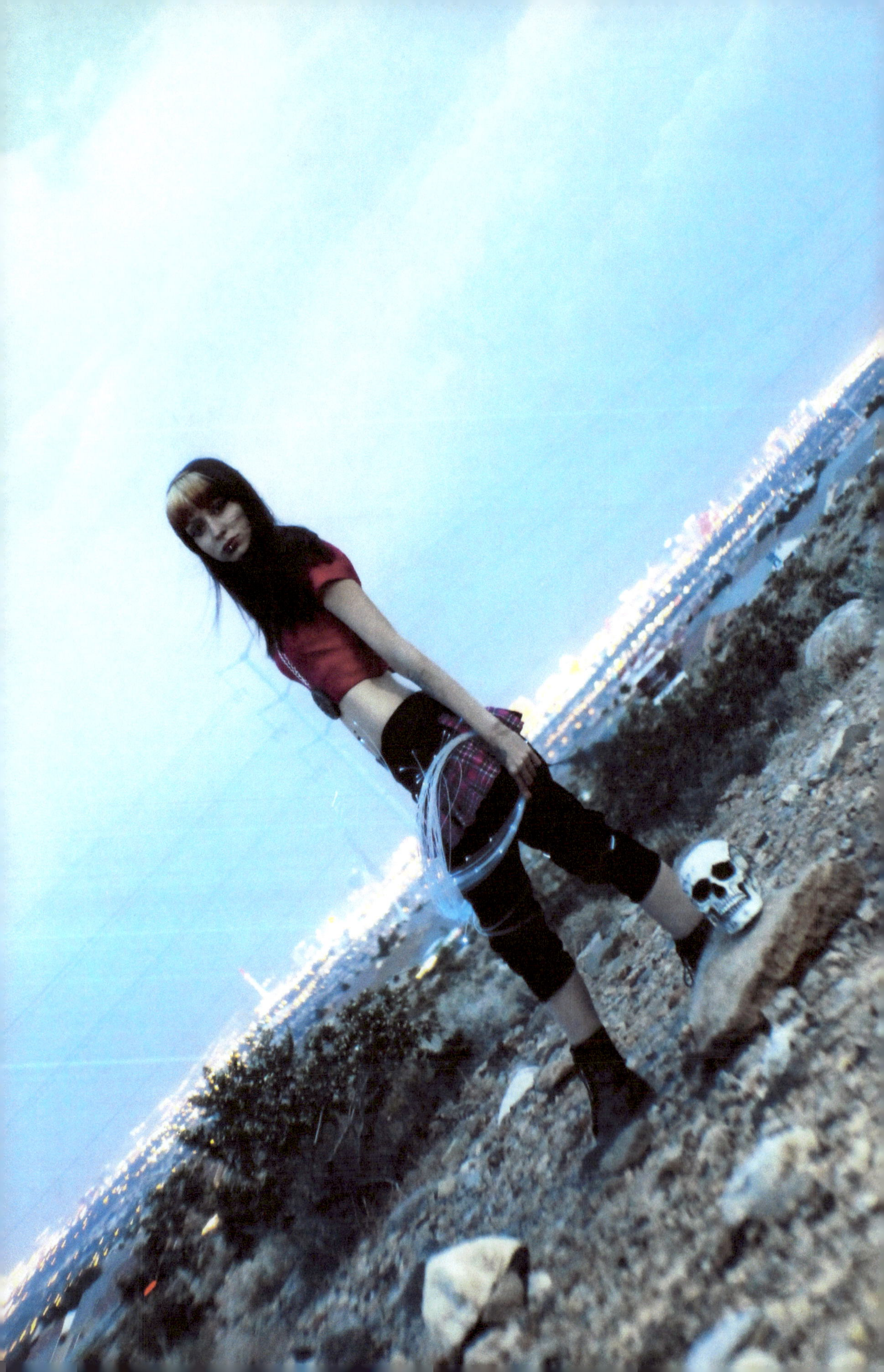

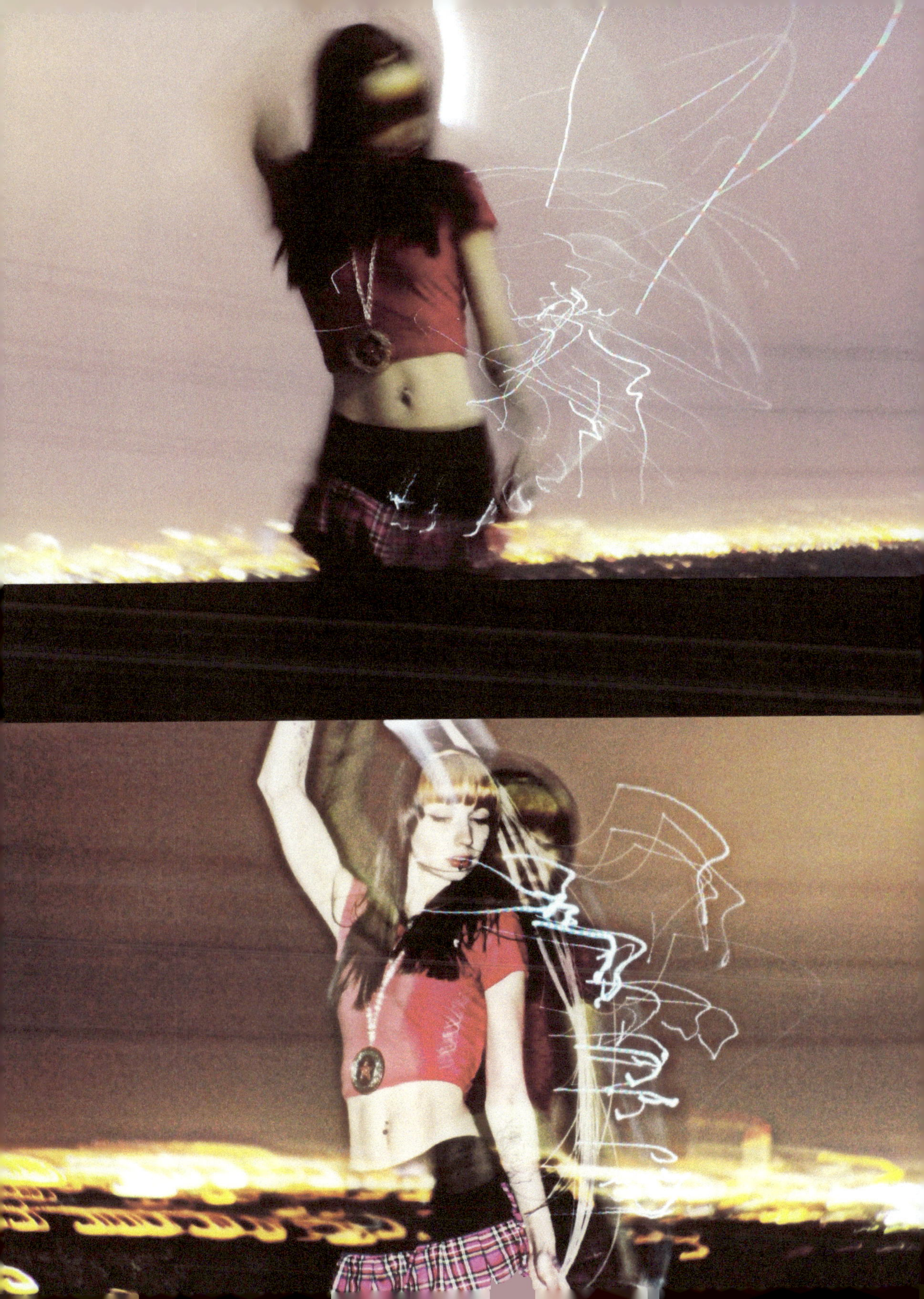

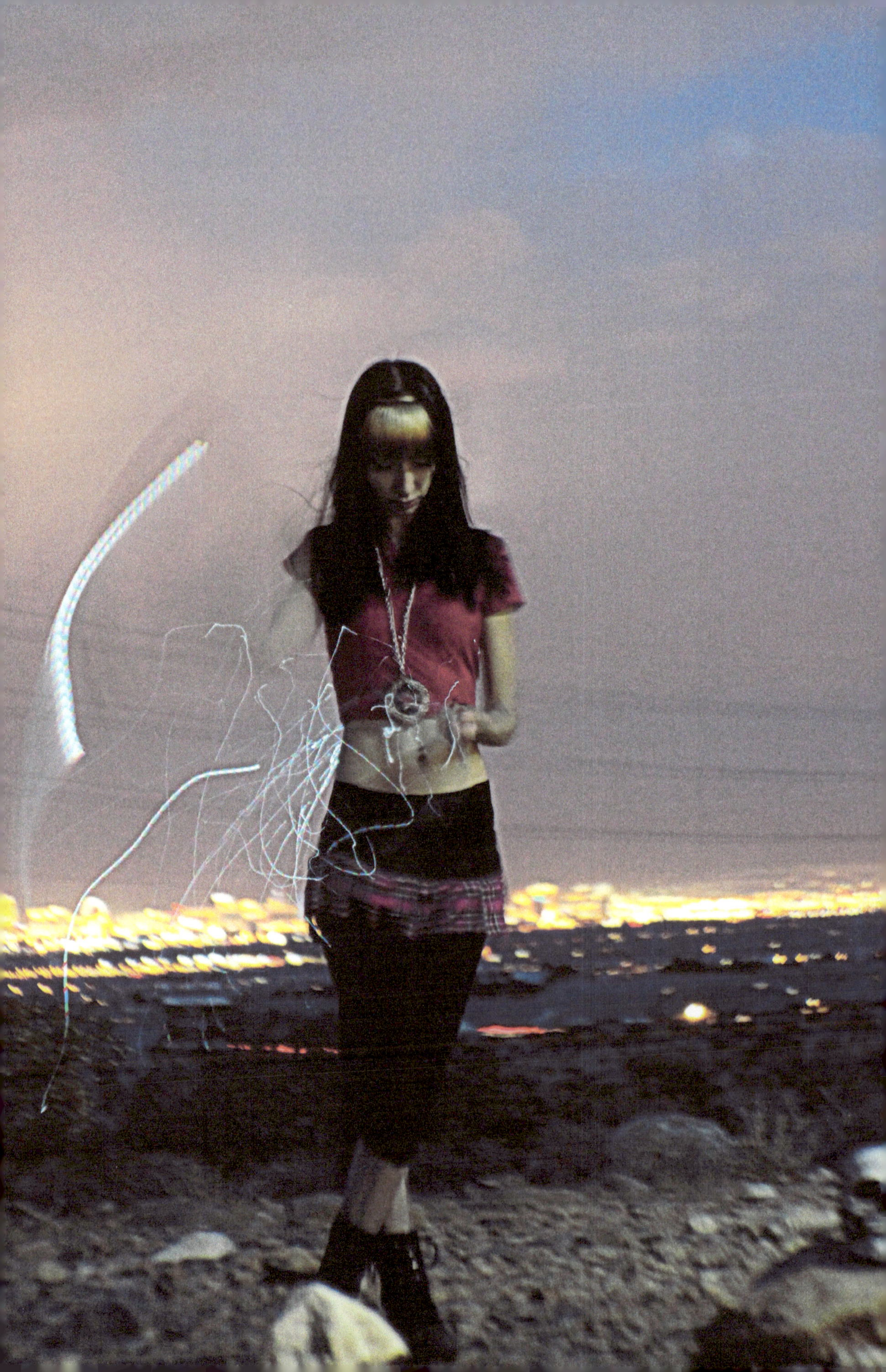

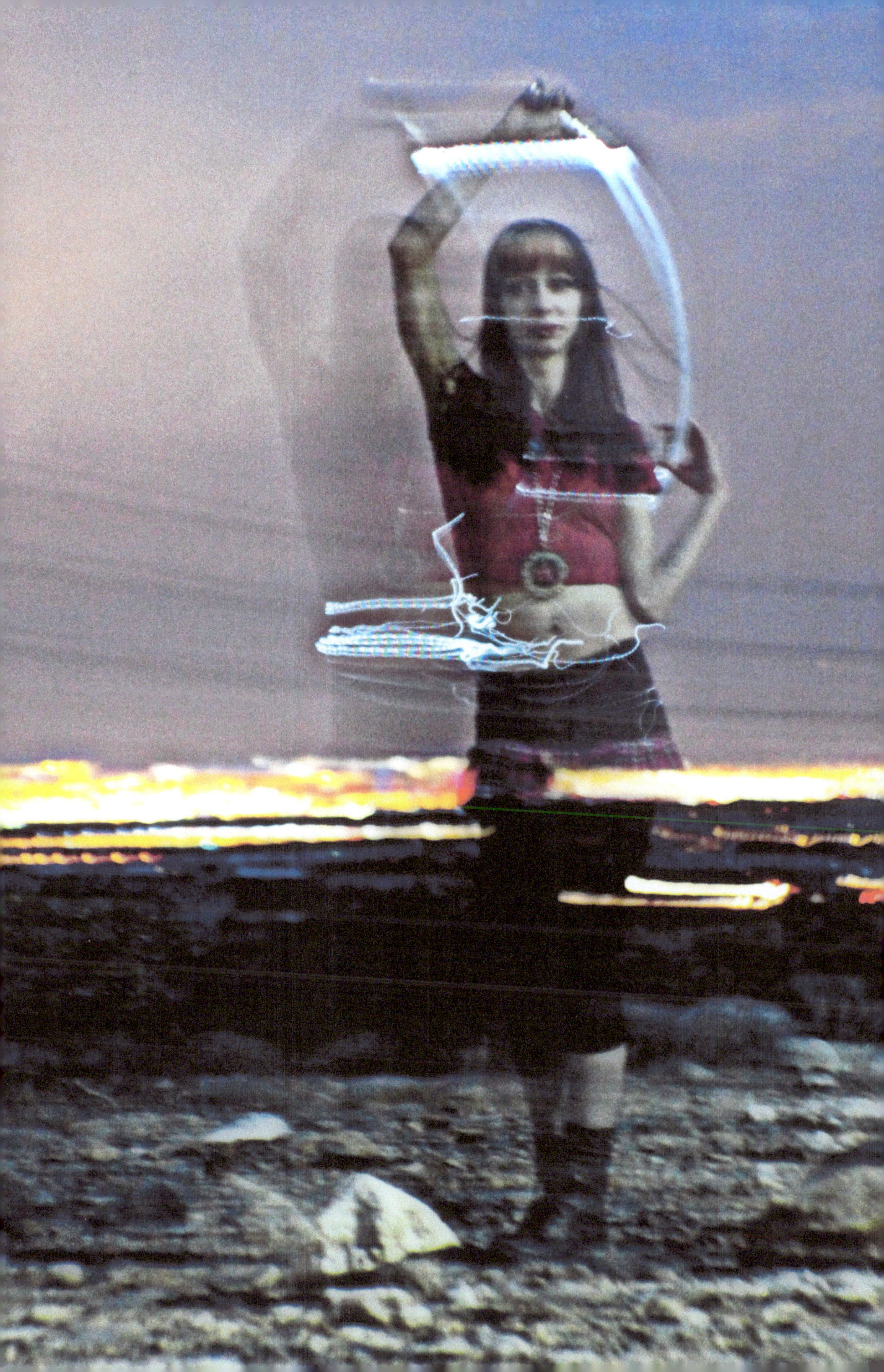

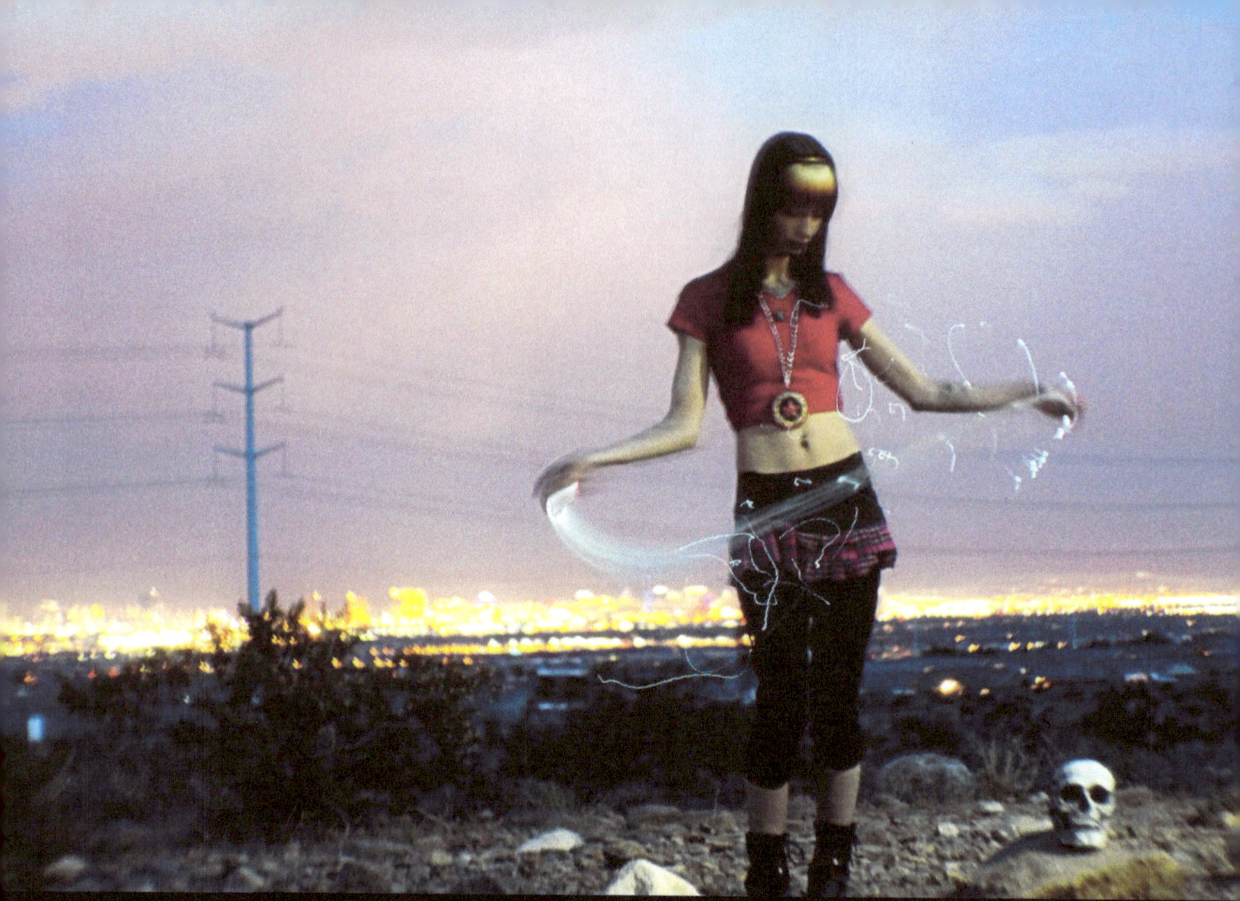

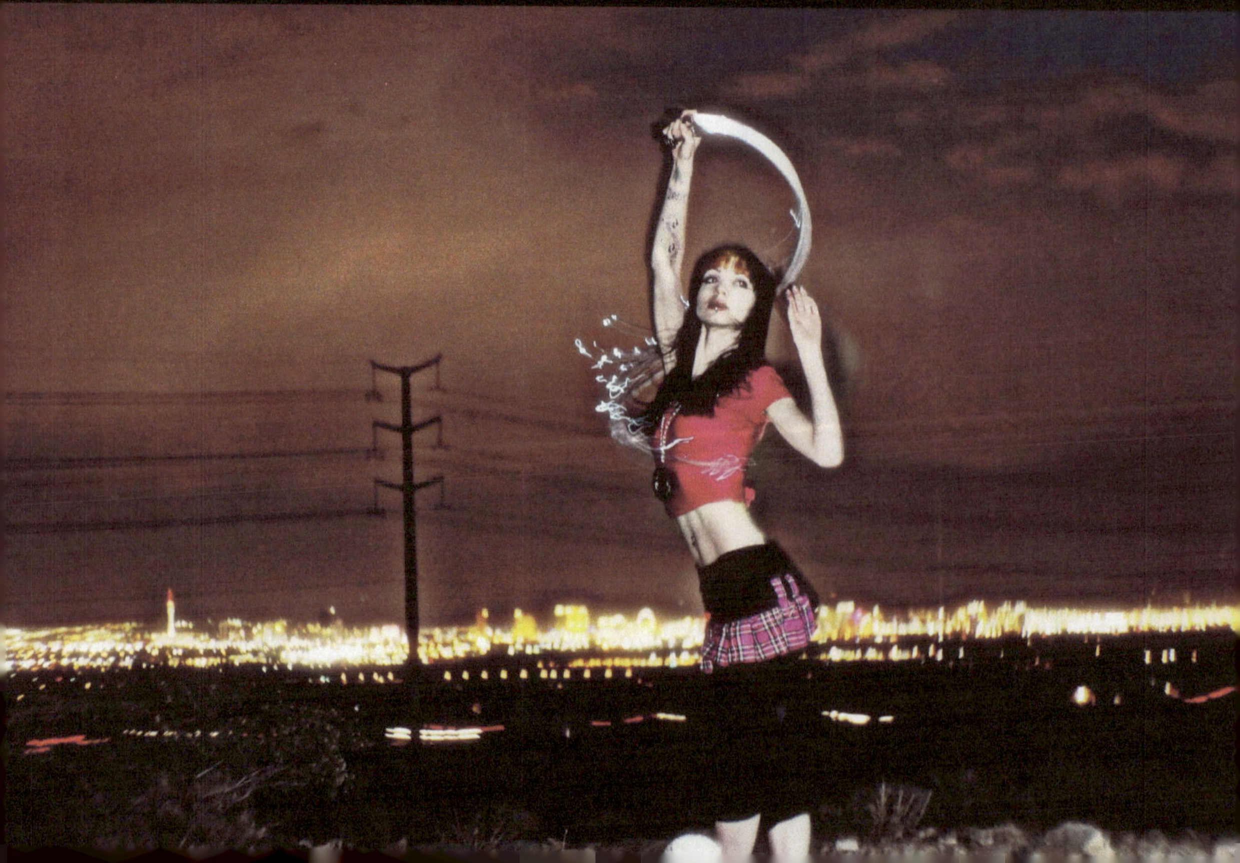

www.ingramcontent.com/pod-product-compliance
Lightning Source LLC
Chambersburg PA
CBHW051107180526
45172CB00002B/804
* 9 7 8 1 5 4 6 5 0 6 2 9 4 *